Bureau of Land Management and the United States Forest Service

Interagency
Smokejumper
Pilots
Operations
Guide

2006 edition: Valid until replaced by a subsequently published edition

Office of Fire and Aviation

This document supersedes the 2005 ISPOG. Valid until replaced by a subsequently published edition

The primary distribution of this Interagency Guide is electronic and can be found at
http://aviation.blm.gov or www.oas.gov
For comments and questions please contact the the BLM or USFS:

> **Office of Fire and Aviation**
> 3833 South Development
> Boise, Idaho 83705

Intentional Left Blank

AMC

INTERAGENCY AVIATION MANAGEMENT COUNCIL

To: User of the *Interagency Smokejumper Pilot Operations Guide*

From: Interagency Aviation Management Council

Date: May 6, 2003

Subject: Publication of 2003 *Interagency Smokejumper Pilot Operations Guide* (ISPOG)

The ISPOG has been revised for new publication in 2003. Changes include revisions proposed by the Smokejumper and Pilot Community, coordinated by the Aviation Management Council (AMC) and approved by the Forest Service and the Department of the Interior in May 2003.

We are confident that the 2003 version of the ISPOG provides the necessary changes identified by field personnel and agency program managers. The ISPOG is a dynamic document, and work will begin immediately to prepare for the next revision.

Copies of this memo will be included at the front of the 2003 ISPOG.

Michael Martin
Acting Director
Office of Aircraft Services
Department of the Interior

Tony Kern
Assistant Director
Aviation & Fire Management
USDA Forest Service

Table of Contents

Chapter

1.0 Introduction

1.1 INTRODUCTION

The Bureau of Land Management and United States Forest Service (USDI/USDA) have developed this information for the guidance of their employees and contractors. The use of trade, firm, or corporation names, or illustrations of any particular product in this publication, is for the information and convenience of the reader and does not constitute an endorsement by the agency of any product, service, or aircraft make and model to the exclusion of others that may be suitable.

This guide is, to a large extent, a compilation of handbooks and guides from various Forest Service regions and BLM bases dating back several spent in developing these previous guidelines, and that expertise is acknowledged and appreciated. For the BLM, this guide replaces the following: DOI Smokejumper Pilots Operations Guide (1999, 2000 and 2001), the BLM New Smokejumper Pilot Orientation Program (1989), the Alaska Smokejumper Project Pilot Handbook (1994), the BLM Fixed Wing Aviation Standard Operatons Procedures, the Pilot's Handbook for Smokejumper and Mountain Flying with the U.S. Forest Service (1986, 1988), USFS 5709.11-22.31 exhibit 1, 5709.11-22.32, exhibit 1, 5709.11-45, 5709.11-43, 44, USFS Smokejumper Pilot Training Guide (1987), and the original OAS Flight Check Guide (Smokejumping/Paracargo). For the USFS this guide supplements pertinent sections of the following Handbooks: 5709.16 Fixed Wing Operations Handbook. 5709.14 Smokejumper/Paracargo Handbook.

A smokejumper aircraft assigned to support wildland fire activity will be utilized in a variety of operations. These may consist of transportation, reconnaissance, airdrop, or jumper retrieval. These operations for the most part will be short-range missions from a main operations base. It is common practice to assign an aircraft to an airport that is adjacent to the area to be covered. Many of these airfields and the communities they serve have been long established as seasonal operating bases by the USFS or BLM, and facilities have been years. There has been much time and effort constructed to accommodate aviation and fire management personnel and equipment.

Many of these airports in the lower 48 are located near high, rugged terrain, radio navigation aids in these areas are often very limited. Good working knowledge of the terrain is helpful. GPS, INS, and other sophisticated navigational equipment may be used routinely and fire dispatches normally include latitude/longitude coordinates.

Flight crews are required to have a good working knowledge of the required navigation systems in their aircraft.On most flights there will be spotter on board who is usually very familiar with the particular Forest or District. However, flight crews still need a working knowledge and understanding of radio communications and frequencies to efficiently complete the mission.

1.2 REVIEWS AND REVISION

Users are encouraged to recommend changes to this document through their respective aviation program manager. The Approving Authority will review this document annually. At that time, appropriate changes will be made. Interim revisions may be issued at any time through the National Aviation Office, and every effort will be made by that office to ensure that these revisions are issued in a timely and coordinated manner.

The guide and revisions are available for ordering through the National Aviation office in Boise, Idaho. The target group for distribution includes users and managers of smokejumper aircraft, smokejumper bases, and smokejumper aircraft contractors

For comments, corrections, additions or general feedback please contact:
ISPOG Steering Committee:

Ron Barrett , USFS	rbarrett01@fs.fed.us	541 - 504 -7260
Scott Curtis, USFS	scurtis@fsfed.us	208 - 387-5882
Gordon Harris	gharris@fs.fed.us	208 - 387- 5637
Ben Hinkle, BLM	ben_hinkle@nifc.blm.gov	208 - 387-5184
Jerff Cardin	Jeff_Cardin@oas.gov	208 - 387-5078
(Advisory / Courtesy)		
Randy Leypoldt	twnpups@aol.com	307- 672-3421
(Advisory / Big Horn Airways/Vendor / **Courtesy**)		

Primary distribution of this document is *electronic* but copies of this publication may be requestedfrom either the BLM or USFS
National Interagency Fire Center
Office of Fire and Aviation
3833 South Development Avenue
Boise, Idaho 83705

1.3 OBJECTIVES

This guide has been prepared to familiarize pilots with the recommended procedures for operating aircraft in the smokejumper and paracargo mission. In the lower 48 states, this includes mountain flying and backcountry airstrip techniques, although general in nature, some specific recommended parameters and configurations for specific aircraft are included in the appendix. Also included is an initial and recurrent pilot training syllabus, including training and evaluation standards and forms.

Chapter
2

2.0 Smokejumper Operations

2.1 GENERAL

The smokejumpers primary mission is to parachute into remote mountain areas to suppress small forest fires before they grow to destructive proportions. Fixed-wing aircraft of various types are their primary transportation to the fire locations. Upon locating the fire, smokejumpers and their equipment are dropped by parachute. When the fire has been extinguished, the smokejumpers proceed on foot to the nearest road, helispot, or airstrip to obtain transportation home. In many cases, the same airplane they parachuted from will return to a nearby airfield several days later to bring them back. Smokejumpers are usually dispatched in multiples of two, rarely singly. The size of the fire, its growth potential, location, and resource reserves are factors that determine how many jumpers are to be dropped to a fire. This consequently dictates the aircraft dispatched to that specific fire. If the fire has been staffed in the meantime, or if it cannot be located, the aircraft is often diverted to another location. This subsequent action will be coordinated by radio with the dispatcher.

A similar situation often arises when multiple fires are spotted or suspected in a given area. Larger aircraft (or several aircraft) loaded to capacity to accomplish multiple drops to several fires will be dispatched. The location of each fire is normally reported to the dispatcher by the spotter on board the aircraft and a determination made as to the order and method in which they are to be handled. Frequently, when multiple fires occur and more severe burning conditions exist, an aerial observer in another aircraft establishes the priority in which the smokejumpers will be utilized. While the spotter on board the aircraft is in control of the mission the pilot is in charge of safely handling the aircraft, therefore there is a continuing need for coordination and communication between the spotter and pilot throughout the flight. As the missions become more complex, it is necessary to share the communications workload in a preplanned manner that allows the fires to be staffed rapidly and efficiently, and provides adequate air traffic separation with other aircraft in the area.

2.2 SPOTTING

Spotting consists of the effective and efficient management of the fire portion of all smokejumper missions to include communication with firefighters and land managers and the safe deployment of smokejumpers and paracargo. This entails determining wind direction and wind velocity by dropping a set of crepe paper " drift streamers" weighted to drift and descend at the same rate as a round parachute. With this technique, a spotter can determine the correct "exit point" over which the jumpers should exit the aircraft to compensate for wind drift so they can land on a preselected jump spot; then guide the pilot to that exit point.

On the first streamer pass, the spotter releases the streamers directly above the desired jump spot. The streamers land downwind, establishing wind drift and direction. The spotter reads the drift and selects the jumper exit point upwind from the jump spot equal distance to the streamer drift. A set of check streamers may be dropped over the exit point, and they should drift back and land close to the jump spot. The jump run pass will normally be made flying into the wind in line over the streamers to the jump spot, then to the exit point.

2.3 RESPONSIBILITIES

2.3.1 THE SPOTTER

1. **Selects the jump spot**, analyzes the conditions, orients the jumpers, and directs the pilot over the point of exit.
2. Coordinates with the pilot to drop the cargo in a selected spot.
3. Discharges the cargo on the pilot's command.
4. Ascertains the welfare of the jumpers and equipment.
5. May, based on observations of the behavior of the fire, take additional or alternative action.
6. May be assigned duties as loadmaster/attendant for passenger hauls per USFS or BLM NAO guidlines.
7. Takes requests from dispatch.
8. Aids in Navigatation to the fire using aeronautical or local maps and GPS.
9. Updates fire coordinates.
10. May be responsible for air traffic control when Air Attack, Lead or ASM is not in the area.
11. Gives fire size up/fire behavior to responsible agency fire management personnel.
12. Coordinates with other resourses on the ground. (i.e. IC, Smokejumpers, crews, etc.)

2.3.2 THE PILOT

1. **Has primary responsibility** in all matters of flight safety.
2. Ensures that all firefighters and cargo are properly loaded.
3. Analyzes weather and flight conditions.
4. Monitors all navigation and activities performed by other crewmembers.
5. Determines if all requested operations can be safely accomplished.
6. Makes the final decision on all drop patterns and cargo placement after consulting with the spotter and/or other resourses on the ground.
7. Selects the cargo drop pattern and gives the kick command.

2.4 DROPPING SMOKEJUMPERS

Aerial delivery of personnel and equipment into small, open spots in steep, forested terrain requires pinpoint accuracy. Excellent crew coordination and sound judgment must be used if these activities are to be accomplished safely and effectively.

The flight crew should ready the aircraft as soon as possible after reporting for duty. Pre-flight and First Flight of Day checklists should be completed. Quick turn checklists should be used whenever authorized.

2.4.1 LOADING AND UNLOADING SMOKEJUMPERS

Smokejumpers may be loaded or unloaded from the jump airplane with the right engine running (multiengine aircraft only). The following procedures must be followed:
1. It must be daylight.
2. One pilot must remain in the left seat at all times.
3. The spotter directs the loading of the smokejumpers, but may delegate the responsibility to ground personnel. The spotter should never leave the aircraft with jumpers on board or engines running without first informing the pilot.
4. If specific agency policy conflicts with the above that agency policy must be followed.

2.4.2 ENROUTE

Flight crews should use the most direct route possible while never compromising safety. A radio call to the IC or other aircraft and lights on are required at least 12 miles from the fire (See Fire Traffic Area Chapter 5.2), as well as completion of mission checklists prior to reaching the fire. Aircraft responding to or operating over wildland fire operations should use the 1255 transponder code unless otherwise instructed by ATC.

2.4.3 MANEUVERING

The pilot must maneuver the aircraft in a manner to provide the spotter and smokejumpers with an unobstructed view of the fire and the surrounding area. This is usually best accomplished by establishing a left hand orbit approximately 1500 feet above the fire and the jump spot. After selecting the area in which jumpers will be dropped, the spotter will identify it to the pilot. The pilot can plan the final approach into the direction of the wind unless terrain features or visibility restrictions make this unsafe, and should make all turns toward the exit side of the aircraft. Any change from a standard into the wind pattern should be agreed on by the pilot and spotter. This allows the spotter to observe the intended jump spot and the behavior of streamers and jumpers during their exit, descent, and landing. Such a pattern also helps to orient the jumpers in the aircraft as to the location of the fire in relation to the jump spot and general lay of the country. Drift streamers are used to test the wind for direction, velocity, updrafts, and downdrafts.

2.4.4 LOW PASS

While it may be omitted, at the discretion of the spotter, in some situations, a low pass (200-500' AGL) may be made at moderate airspeed over the selected jump spot .
The low pass allows good size up of the fire, jump spot, hazards, and wind conditions as *well* as a confirmation of altitude with radar altimeter.

2.4.5 STREAMER LINE UP

The pilot should plan the turns so that the aircraft will be lined up on a wings level final at 1500' AGL optimally 10-15 seconds from drop. The pilot verbally informs the spotter "on final, jumpers / streamers XXXAGL" The spotter gives voice commands to the pilot to correct either to the left or right. These direction changes will be coordinated standard rate turns, and are normally 5 degrees unless specified by the spotter. The pilot should use terrain as the primary reference for direction of flight. The directional gyro is a secondary reference. Altitude must be held constant. The spotter may request altitude changes, however, based on rising terrain at the exit point or beyond. Such changes are usually voiced as "up 200'", etc. Two streamer passes are generally made.

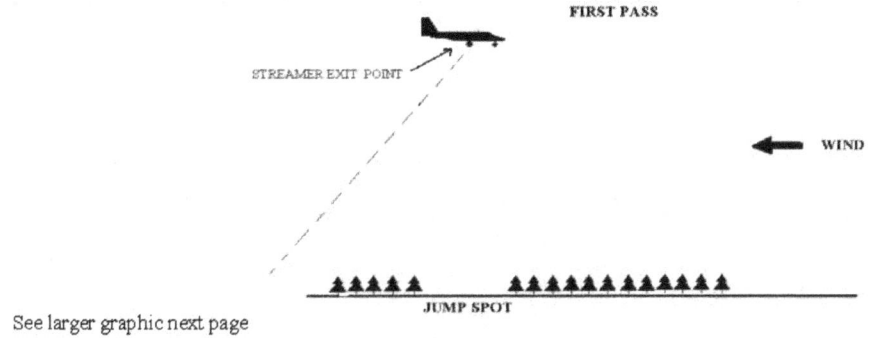

See larger graphic next page

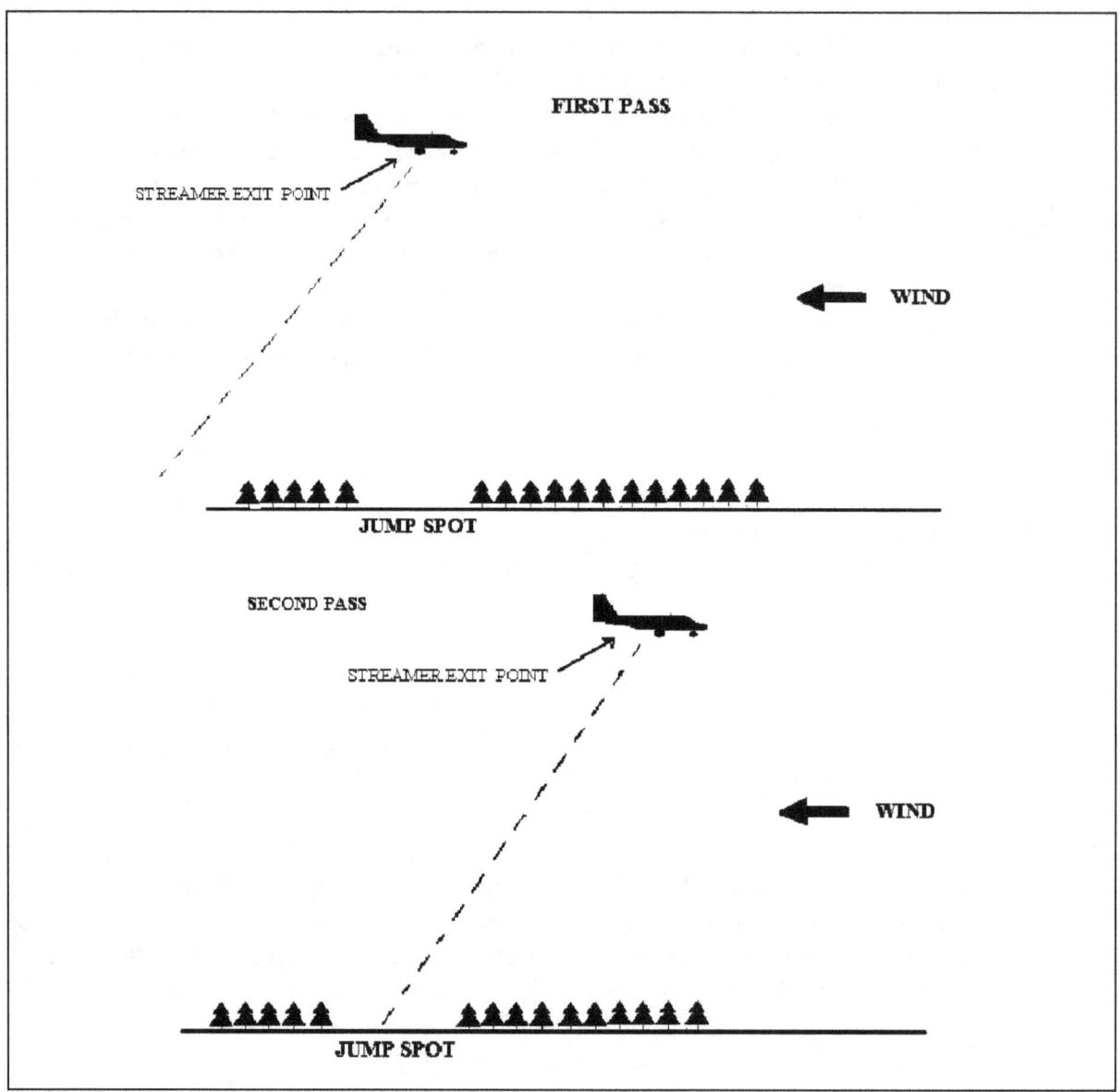

2.4.6 DROPPING STREAMERS

Upon the call from the spotter, "streamers away", the pilot shall respond wth the altiutde shown on the radar altimeter and begin a turn into the direction of the open door at a bank angle commensurate with the type and speed of the aircraft (approximately 30 degrees, not to exceed 45 degrees). Transport Category aircraft should not routinely exceed 30 degrees of bank. Bank angles approaching 45 degrees are stiuations which call "watch out". It is of primary importance that the spotter be able to observe the streamers at all times, as he is determining wind drift, vertical air currents, ground winds, and exit point. If the view is blanked out by the wing or fuselage for longer than a few seconds it may be impossible to relocate them. The Pilot must be able to locate the streamers for subsequent streamer and jump passes.

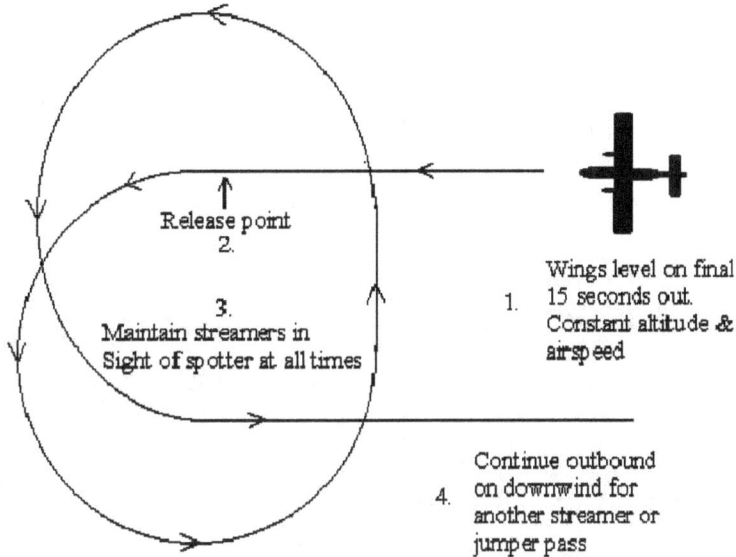

Release point
2.

3.
Maintain streamers in
Sight of spotter at all times

Wings level on final
15 seconds out.
Constant altitude &
airspeed

1.

Continue outbound
on downwind for
another streamer or
jumper pass

4.

Steep turns cause the wing to blank out the streamers to the smokejumpers as well. If their exact point of impact cannot be determined, a "pass" is wasted. Under normal conditions, at least two streamer passes are made (the second being a "check set"). A change in final approach direction may be requested if the spotter deems it necessary.

The spotter will be timing the descent of the streamers to measure vertical and horizontal air movement (Usually 65-70 seconds in vertically calm air). Short descents may indicate dangerous downdrafts which may preclude dropping jumpers or necessitate changing jump spots.

2.4.7 DROPPING JUMPERS:

When the spotter is satisfied that all conditions are satisfactory, the spotter informs the pilot that jumpers will be dropped on the next pass. The procedure is the same as that used for dropping streamers (except that a climb to 3000 feet AGL is necessary for ram air chutes) , with the same same airspeed as used on the streamer pass, except for slowing on final to achieve 1.3 Vso at the exit point for the jumpers . A standard pattern can be established as illustrated below. **Occasionally,** topographical, hazards, such as a large river, make it desirable to deviate from a normal into-the-wind pattern when dropping jumpers. In some cases a crosswind, downwind, or righthand pattern may be requested (nonstandard). See the next page.

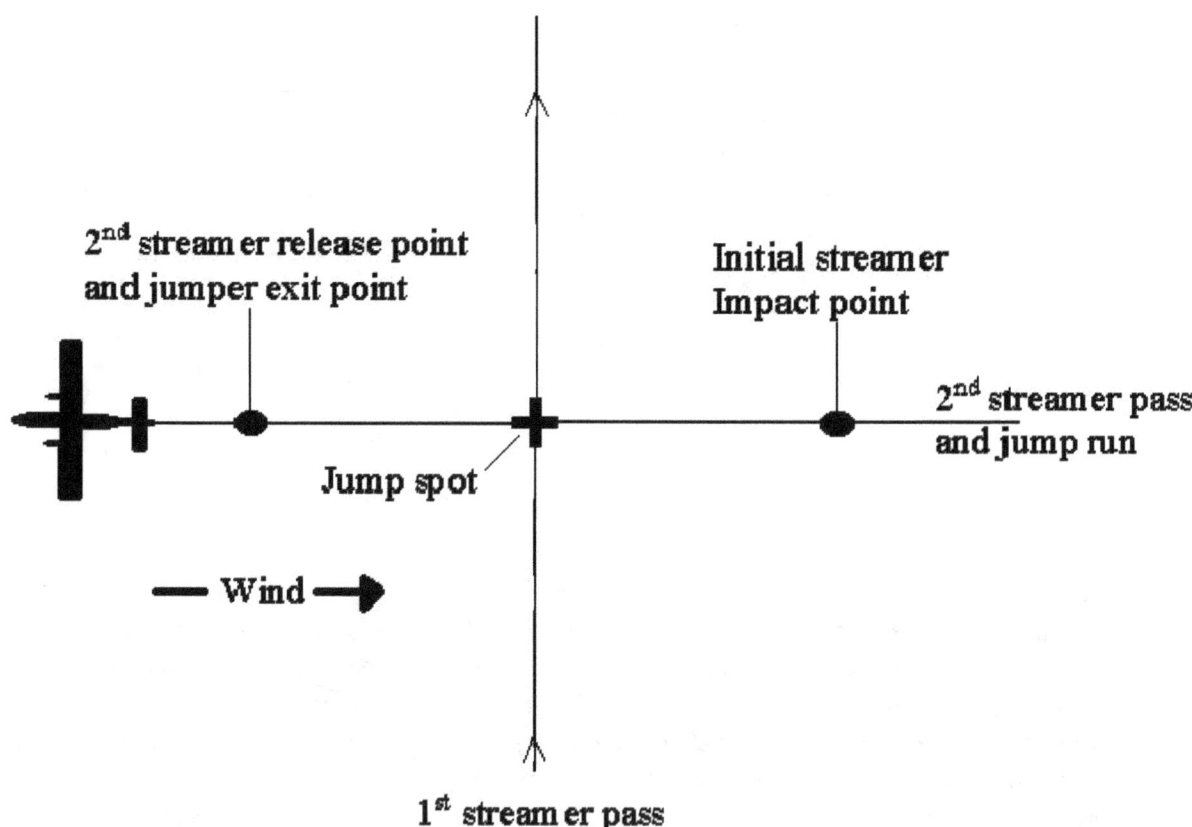

NON STANDARD CROSSWIND PATTERN

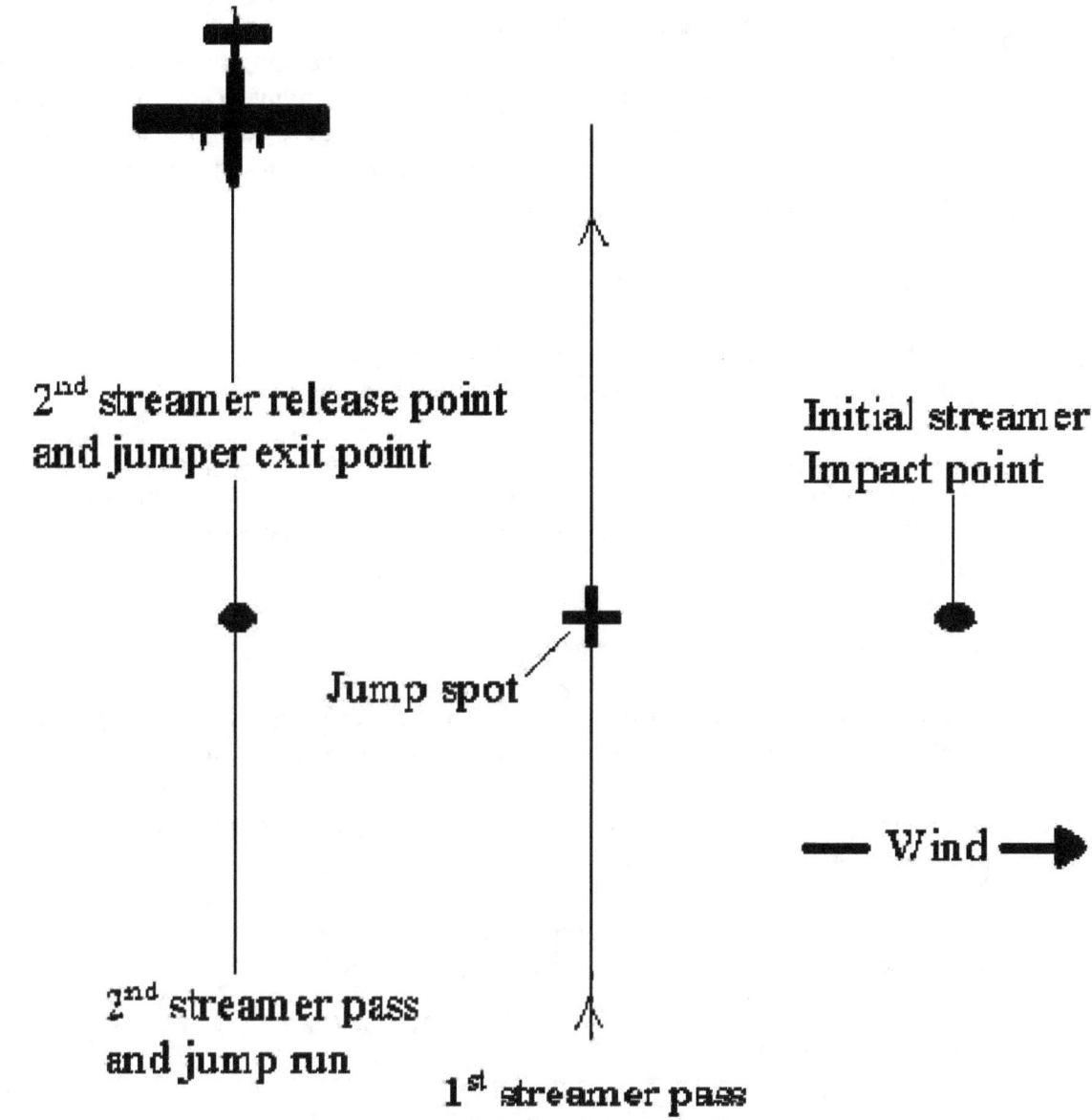

2nd streamer release point
and jumper exit point

Initial streamer
Impact point

Jump spot

Wind

2nd streamer pass
and jump run

1st streamer pass

2.4.8 SIGNALING

The spotter calls "jumper away" after each jumper or stick of jumpers has cleared the aircraft. The pilot maintains aircraft heading and airspeed until receiving this command. A turn is then begun (standard pattern) in the direction of the jump door (20 to 30 degree's bank) to the downwind heading. The ideal pattern should allow for no more that a 30 degree bank with enough time on final for the spotter to determine the correct line up and give corrections. The pilot should call downwind and turning base. When established on final the pilot will call "on final jumpers xxxx feet Agl".

2.4.9 COMMUNICATIONS

Spotter technique varies with the individual. One person may be satisfied with a long final approach and another may request the pilot to shorten the pattern.

Good communication and coordination (CRM) is essential between pilot and spotter if a mission is to be accomplished effectively. The operation will always run more smoothly if intentions and problems are thoroughly discussed and understood by both parties before, during, and after the drop.

2.4.10 CHECKING JUMPERS

When the drop has been completed and all personnel are on the ground, the spotter ascertains, via radio with the smokejumper in charge, that there are no injuries. Occasionally radios may be damaged in the drop, but it is rare that voice communication cannot be established. If necessary, visual signals may be used. In any case, communications must be established before starting the paracargo drop.

The spotter may choose to establish communication with the first stick of jumpers before dropping more personnel. This is to verify the exit point and selection of jump spot.

2.4.11 ALTITUDES

a. **Absolute minimum altitudes** are **1500' AGL** for round chutes and **3000' AGL** for squares. Jump Altitude is the altitude above the exit point, not the altitude above the jump spot. In many cases the exit point upwind of the jump spot will be higher or lower terrain than the jump spot. This difference in terrain elevation must be taken into account when establishing drop pattern altitude. Exit point altitude is usually never lower than the minimum drop altitudes over the DZ. Pilots should look ahead and anticipate this factor when selecting an altitude prior to streamer dropping. Spotters should point out high terrain upwind of the jump spot to the pilot and request extra altitude. Lower terrain upwind does NOT imply that jump altitude must also be lower than 1500' or 3000' above the jumpspot.

b. **Radar altimeters** should be used whenever possible to determine altitude. This readout should be communicated to the spotter after the call "streamers away". Since some radar altimeters don't register to 3000' AGL, simple math must be used to calculate the proper barometric altimeter readout. All altitude callouts to the spotter are in AGL, not MSL.

2.4.12 JUMP ALTITUDES

Operational smokejumping altitudes are a compromise between best accuracy and maximizing time available for reserve procedures. Anti-inversion nets were attached to the skirts of round parachutes in 1978. Their malfunction rate since is Near a zero. The US military routinely drops paratroopers on such canopies at 500 feet AGL. These are combat simulation jumps. Their rationale - avoidance of lethal unfriendly gunfire is more critical to troop survival than having sufficient altitude to accomplish reserve procedures.

Hitting a small jumpspot in rugged terrain often is a primary concern of smokejumpers. The ability to deploy a reserve parachute in the event of a malfunctioned main is of primary importance. Our standard operational altitudes were derived from analysis of actual reserve parachute deployments in sport, military, and smokejumping events or operations. On either canopy system, jumpers could depart the aircraft at any higher-than-standard altitude and have even more time available for reserve procedures in the event of a malfunction or failure to hook up. We normally do not because.
1. More time spent under canopy would delay action on fire.
2. Other air traffic near the fire could be confused, and
3. Jumpers could land scattered over a larger area delaying fire action.
4. Safety is not compromised.

2.4.13 MINIMUM PULL ALTITUDE

For either type of reserve, 400 ft (AGL) is the absolutely lowest altitude at which a jumper may reasonably expect the result of reserve activation to cause both deployment and deceleration prior to impact.

A round jumper who fails to hook up will fall from 1500 ft to 400 ft in about 10 seconds. A ram air jumper who fails to hook up (or fails to pull the drogue release handle) will drop from 3000 ft to 400 ft in about 19 seconds.

2.4.14 DROP ALTITUDE

Drop altitude is measured from the aircraft to the ground directly below WHEN & WHERE the jumpers exit. It could be substantially different than the elevation above the jumpspot.

2.4.15 PRACTICE AND DEMONSTRATION JUMPS

There is no protection under public aircraft law for practice or demonstration jumps. The PIC is responsible under FAR part 91 and 105. Please refer to the FARS and Advisory Circular 105.2C for proper guidance. You may also use this BLM adaptation of Advisory Circular 105.2C.

Practice – Demonstration Jump Airspace NOTAM Flow Chart				
Location of Jump	Kind of Authorization Required	When to Apply or Notify	Where to Apply and Notify	FAR Section Reference
Over or into a congested area or open air assembly of persons	FAA Form 7711-2	Apply at least 4 working days before the jump.	FSDO having jurisdiction over the area where jump is to be made	105.15
Over or onto an airport with or without a US operated control tower.	Prior Approval	Apply before the jump. **	Airport Management	105.17
In or into a control zone with a US. Operated control tower.	Authorization (verbal can be used)	Apply before the jump. **	ATC Tower having jurisdiction over the control zone *	105.19
In or onto an airport with a radar service area	Authorization (verbal can be used)	Apply before the jump. **	ATC tower at the airport for which the airport radar service area is designated.	105.20
Into or within a positive control area or terminal control area	Authorization (verbal can be used)	Apply before the jump. **	Nearest FAA ATC facility or FSS. *	105.21
In or into other controlled airspace.	None	1 hour before the jump is made but not more than 24 hours before jumping is to be completed. **	Nearest FAA ATC facility or FSS.	105.23
Jump over or with restricted or prohibited areas.	Authorization (verbal can be used)	Apply before the jump. **	The agency in charge of the area.	105.27
* Communication is required with the nearest FAA ATC facility or FSS 5 minutes before the jump. **BLM Aviation desires NOTAMS to be filed 24 hours in advance.				

Chapter

3

3.0 Paracargo

3.1 NORMAL

Normally, cargo dropping operations will not begin until all jumpers are known to be safely on the ground in known positions.

After the last jumper has exited, the spotter readies the cargo for dropping and should confer with the pilot and the jumper in charge on the ground as to the desired and most practical place to drop the bundles. The spotter will normally inform the pilot of cargo type and number of pallets/bundles to be dropped and the size of the canopy. The pilot shall carefully analyze the terrain and conditions in relation to the desired impact area, and make a dry run in all but the easiest drop areas.

The pilot should notify the spotter when on each pattern leg, i.e. downwind, base, and final. Five to ten seconds from the release point the pilot will state "short final" followed by "standby" and "kick" when over the release point.

The spotter may request that the pass be made at a higher altitude in order to give the parachute more time to deploy. In most cases, the pilot will need to devote full attention to flying the aircraft in order to clear obstructions and will be unable to observe the parachute until on the downwind or final portion of the pattern.

Cargo drops will normally he made at a minimum altitude of approximately 150' AGL to 200 AGL' (radar altimeters will not account for tree height). The chutes need time to fully open and to decelerate. At the discretion of the pilot, the cargo may be dropped at a higher altitude.

3.2 EXTRA HEAVY BUNDLES

Specially rigged parachutes, turbulence, restricted visibility, timberlines or other terrain features and other considerations may dictate such change. In steep topography patterns are often flown down the ridge (or parallel)to prevent cargo that is released long or short from floating down into canyon bottoms.

The importance of carefully and accurately analyzing the terrain, other obstructions and wind effect before committing yourself on a low-altitude cargo pass cannot be over-emphasized. This size up should be ongoing from the initial pass over the fire. There are very few occasions on an actual fire drop where conditions will be ideal, and each mission will vary in some respects. A low-altitude cargo pass should never be made into the face of a mountain or up a canyon where maximum power or a very steep turn will be required to clear obstructions (no uphill finals) . The pilot shall plan the pattern so that the ground level falls away after the bundle has been dispatched, so that a minimum of maneuvering is necessary to put the aircraft over lower terrain.

3.3 CARGO DROPS

Cargo drops are often required in the very bottom of steep and winding canyons where a turn into the wrong drainage could result in a dead end. Always leave yourself a way to turn out in case of down drafts, turbulence, engine failure, or the off chance of a bundle hanging up on the tail of the aircraft. Consideration should be given to impact points on bundels being cut away.

If the cargo is hung in the trees climbing spurs will be deployed by free fall. Free fall items are not attached to parachutes. They may include sleeping bags and various hand tools, but most often climbers. The technique is basically the same as paracargo deployment, except the dissimilar trajectory must be taken into account, plus the fact that there may be considerable ground travel of the spurs after impact.

3.4 FREE-FALLING CARGO

Free-falling cargo is also extremely hazardous to ground personnel; it is therefore incumbent upon the pilot making such drops to suspend the operation if anything looks unsafe, and notify the ground personnel by radio of the free fall cargo. Climbing spurs are dangerous due to the possibility of ricochet in a heavy timber area. It is good technique to drop from a slightly higher altitude to dissipate some of the horizontal trajectory vector.

It is important for a pilot to use all his skill and talent to develop cargo accuracy. Terrain can be very difficult to walk in and major exertion is required to pack a 90-135 lb. cargo bundle. Remember that at 90-100 KIAS, you are traveling about 50 yards per second. One second too soon or too late can easily put cargo in the trees.

3.5 LOW LEVEL ASSESMENT TABLES. DC 3/DHC-6/SHERPA

DOES NOT PROVIDE SINGLE ENGINE PERFORMANCE!

- **DC3**

NOTE: Tabulated data in this document for management tool only. Not to be used for flight planning purposes. Not FAA approved.

DC3-TP67 Pressure Altitude Ceiling to Achieve +0.6% Gross Climb Gradient								
Temp	40c	35c	30c	25c	20c	15c	10c	5c
28,750	1,250	2,310	3,300	4,310	5,000	5,840	6,570	7,290
28,500	1,900	2,630	3,700	5,000	5,440	6,190	6,920	7,690
28,000	2,000	2,890	4,000	5,400	5,600	6,460	7,230	8,000
27,500	3,110	4,000	4,950	5,900	6,720	7,500	8,670	8,920
27,000	3,440	4,430	5,380	6,240	7,040	7,840	8,410	8,900
26,500	3,780	4,840	5,760	6,640	7,460	8,140	8,680	9,190
26,000	4,420	5,380	6,320	6,840	7,920	8,514	9,000	9,550
25,500	4,740	5,750	6,720	7,520	8,270	8,780	9,330	9,890
25,000	N/A	6,210	7,100	8,000	8,560	9,110	9,670	N/A
24,500	N/A	6,800	7,560	8,310	8,860	9,440	10,000	N/A
24,000	N/A	7,100	8,000	8,680	9,290	9,880	N/A	N/A
23,500	N/A	N/A	8,380	9,000	9,610	N/A	N/A	N/A
23,000	N/A	N/A	8,700	9,400	10,000	N/A	N/A	N/A
22,500	N/A	N/A	9,100	9,800	N/A	N/A	N/A	N/A
22,000	N/A	N/A	10,000	N/A	N/A	N/A	N/A	N/A
21,500	N/A	N/A	N/A	N/A	N/A	N/A	N/A	N/A
21,000	N/A	N/A	N/A	N/A	N/A	N/A	N/A	N/A
20,500	N/A	N/A	N/A	N/A	N/A	N/A	N/A	N/A
20,000	N/A	N/A	N/A	N/A	N/A	N/A	N/A	N/A
19,500	N/A	N/A	N/A	N/A	N/A	N/A	N/A	N/A
19,000	N/A	N/A	N/A	N/A	N/A	N/A	N/A	N/A
18,500	N/A	N/A	N/A	N/A	N/A	N/A	N/A	N/A
18,000	N/A	N/A	N/A	N/A	N/A	N/A	N/A	N/A

Aircraft Weight (row labels)

Charts: Second Segment Gross Gradient of Climb, Page 5-27 DC3-TP67 Flight Manual, Report No. ER512-011 FAA Approved 2/27/90.

- Gear UP, Flaps UP, Bleed: Cockpit Heat ON or OFF
- One Engine Inoperative, Propeller Feathered
- Climb Speed: V2 (Ref. Page 5-18)

N/A	Indicates out of range of chart
N/A	Indicates above 10,000' PA, and beyond range of highest PA curve

- **DHC-6** (-27 ENGINES) DOES NOT PROVIDE SINGLE ENGINE PERFORMANCE!

NOTE: Tabulated data in this document for management tool only. Not to be used for flight planning purposes. Not FAA approved.

DHC-6 Pressure Altitude Ceiling to Achieve +0.6% Climb Gradient

Temp	40c	35c	30c	25c	20c	15c	10c	5c
12,500	4,700	6,120	7,250	8,090	8,730	9,480	N/A	N/A
12,000	N/A	6,890	8,000	8,790	10,000	N/A	N/A	N/A
11,500	N/A	N/A	8,880	9,880	N/A	N/A	N/A	N/A
11,000	N/A	N/A	10,000	N/A	N/A	N/A	N/A	N/A
10,500	N/A	N/A	N/A	N/A	N/A	N/A	N/A	N/A
10,000	N/A	N/A	N/A	N/A	N/A	N/A	N/A	N/A
9,500	N/A	N/A	N/A	N/A	N/A	N/A	N/A	N/A
9,000	N/A	N/A	N/A	N/A	N/A	N/A	N/A	N/A
8,500	N/A	N/A	N/A	N/A	N/A	N/A	N/A	N/A
8,000	N/A	N/A	N/A	N/A	N/A	N/A	N/A	N/A
7,500	N/A	N/A	N/A	N/A	N/A	N/A	N/A	N/A
7,000	N/A	N/A	N/A	N/A	N/A	N/A	N/A	N/A

(Aircraft Weight shown on left axis)

Chart used: Take-off Gradient of Climb – One Engine Inoperative
PSM 1-63-1A, Figure 5-11-18, Section 5 page 5-11-4-46

Associated conditions:
Wing flaps   =   Take-off (10°)
Intake deflectors   =   Retracted
Engines   =   One engine inoperative, propeller feathered.
Other engine at take-off power, prop rpm 96%.

- **C-23A/SD3** DOES NOT PROVIDE SINGLE ENGINE PERFORMANCE!

Sherpa Pressure Altitude Ceiling to Achieve +0.6% Gross Climb Gradient

Aircraft Weight

Temp	40c	35c	30c	25c	20c	15c	10c	5c
22,900	3,000	3,990	4,730	5,440	6,130	6,630	7,170	7,670
22,500	3,330	4,240	5,000	5,670	6,300	7,170	7,370	7,870
22,000	4,000	4,800	5,600	6,290	6,820	7,390	7,930	8,470
21,500	4,500	5,330	6,190	6,780	7,330	7,890	8,370	8,900
21,000	5,000	5,800	6,480	7,100	7,720	8,300	8,770	9,270
20,500	N/A	6,500	7,250	7,770	8,410	9,000	9,590	10,000
20,000	N/A	7,130	7,750	8,360	8,890	9,450	10,000	N/A
19,500	N/A	N/A	8,430	9,070	9,540	10,000	N/A	N/A
19,000	N/A	N/A	8,860	9,470	10,000	N/A	N/A	N/A
18,500	N/A	N/A	9,600	10,000	N/A	N/A	N/A	N/A
18,000	N/A	N/A	10,000	N/A	N/A	N/A	N/A	N/A
17,500	N/A	N/A	N/A	N/A	N/A	N/A	N/A	N/A
17,000	N/A	N/A	N/A	N/A	N/A	N/A	N/A	N/A
16,500	N/A	N/A	N/A	N/A	N/A	N/A	N/A	N/A
16,000	N/A	N/A	N/A	N/A	N/A	N/A	N/A	N/A

Charts used: Normal Net Flight Path – Segment 2 Net Climb Gradient- Figure A3-31 T.O. 1C-23A-1 (Reading -0.2% Net Climb Gradient which is equivalent to +0.6% Gross Climb Gradient as per section 6.4, page A3-59)
Green shaded areas are outside of chart boundaries but greater than 10,000' PA, N/A are off chart.
Section 6.4, page A3-59 Net Flight Path paragraph reads as follows:

Net Flight Path

In Normal Operations the gross performance is reduced by a safety margin to obtain net performance. In this manual the gross flight path performance has been reduced by the equivalent of 0.8% climb gradient to obtain net flight path performance. This is the level of performance scheduled for obstacle clearance calculations as required by FAR 25.115 for two engined airplanes.

Chapter

4

4.0 Reconnaissance and Survey

4.1 RECONNAISSANCE OR DETECTION

Reconnaissance or detection flights may be requested on the basis of lightning forecasts and thunderstorm cell development provided by radar and other detection equipment. Reconnaissance missions require competence and judgment on the part of the pilot and the observers. A knowledge of windage, proper mountain flying techniques and terrain flying are necessary. Familiarity with the country is very helpful.

The airplane should be flown to provide the observers with the best possible visibility. Flying should be as smooth as possible to relieve the observers from unnecessary physical strain. The pilot should anticipate the observers, needs, and maneuver the airplane rather than forcing the observers to constantly shift position.

Proposed routes should be laid out on a map for each of the foreseeable conditions that may occur. Systematic profiling of critical points along the proposed route is essential. This permits easier determination of alternate flight routes. Flight routes should be planned to position the observer for best ground observation.

The flight altitude is determined by: Intensity of patrol, amount and altitude of haze, width of observation strip, topography type, amount of cloud and hill shadow, sun angle and direction, background, and minimum altitude for safe flight. Under normal circumstances most flights are conducted at an intermediate altitude because of terrain and fire reconnaissance responsibilities (1500-5000' AGL). Flights shall not be conducted at less than 500 feet above the ground or canopy. Regulations may require flights above 2000' AGL.

If an altitude is selected that will clear all terrain over the path of flight with a minimum of maneuvering to avoid the higher isolated mountain peaks, the pilot and observer obtain optimum visual coverage of the surrounding area. Again, knowledge of the country is important in order to determine the best route in relation to drainage, passes, and higher peaks. Above 3000' AGL, standard FAA cruise altitudes should be used. Slow cruise speed (economy cruise) is best. Under certain conditions, slower speeds may be necessary to adequately observe specific areas. Both high and low speeds have advantages depending on conditions and observation objectives. The pilot should make every effort to maneuver the airplane to provide the best possible view of the terrain. The observers should direct the pilot regarding flight path and will probably request frequent altitude and pattern changes.

Each area should be thoroughly investigated. The flight pattern should be worked out from maps, profiles, and actual flights so all important areas directly visible are fairly close range to the observers. Air observers should continue to refine the patrol routes and make adjustments to the patrol map by the following:

Chapter

5

5.0 COMMUNICATIONS, FIRE TRAFFIC, RESOURCE TRACKING AND FLIGHT FOLLOWING

5.1 COMMUNICATIONS

All aircraft operating under fleet or contract to the USDA/USDI are required to have two VHF transceivers with 760 channel capability and at least one approved FM transceiver. The FM transceiver is the primary communications link for all fire activity. It may also be utilized to communicate with other agencies and aircraft. Instructions and frequency assignments are contained in the agencies radio users guide and Wildland Firefighter Frequency Guide which should be kept in the cockpit of each aircraft in which this unit is installed. Some specific regional frequencies may be included in an appendix to this guide. It is essential that pilots be very familiar with operation of this radio. No aircraft, be it contract, cooperator, news media, or military, will be allowed to operate (or continue to operate) over any fire without an operational radio capable of maintaining clear communication on the assigned frequencies.

All aircraft will identify themselves by make and aircraft "N" number except for air tankers, ASM modules (Helicopter or Fixed Wing) and lead planes who will use their assigned number, and smokejumper aircraft who may use, for example, "Jumper 49". Some regions and agencies assign special numbers to their contract helicopters which can be expected to appear on the scene of any large incident. Other exceptions would be incident overhead who may be airborne in the performance of their duties. They should, in plain language, identify the fact that they are in the air and in what type of aircraft. Examples would be: "This is Sheep Creek Fire Air Attack over the fire at niner thousand in Cessna 42B" or "this is Sheep Creek Fire Command. We have just departed base heliport in helicopter 320 for reconnaissance of the south flank".

The Smokejumper Aircraft Contract requires that audio control panels be installed and operational in the pilot, copilot, and spotters positions. This enables the spotter to communicate directly with the people on the ground or with other aircraft if necessary. Normally the pilots (two pilot crew) will handle all communications with FAA facilities and other aircraft as necessary while the spotter makes routine position reports, ground contact, and other fire related contacts. This does not releive Flight Following responsibiltiy for DOI pilots.

The spotter may handle communications with other fire related aircraft, particularly in single pilot operations. An intercom system allows the pilot and spotter to communicate while in flight and monitor other frequencies at the same time. Considerable preplanning and coordination is needed to enable the pilot to select the required frequencies during the operation and to give proper position and situation reports when the spotter is occupied dropping jumpers and cargo. There often occurs a mix of out-of-area or new spotters flying with pilots who are very familiar with the geographic area of the mission. This situation is also commonly reversed. If either individual is obviously operating in his home territory and the other is not it will improve the quality of the mission if the position reports are given by or relayed from the person who knows the landmarks. This is just good crew resource management.

5.2 FIRE AREA TRAFFIC

Aviation activity over a going fire can become a frantic and hazardous experience if not managed properly. Large fires that have had adequate time to set up the incident command organization should have established the order of work, drop priorities, radio procedures and airspace control. Key points the Fire Traffic Area are an initial call at 12 miles and if no communications are received a hold at 7 miles.

The most critical situation is during the initial attack phase of an emerging fire when several aircraft arrive over the scene at almost the same time. The order of authority for air traffic control and drop or mission priorities is as follows: 1, ATGS, 2. ASM/LeadPlane 3. Smokejumper Spotter.

All pilots should have received information regarding air or ground contact and radio frequencies with their dispatch instructions. When approaching a fire that is already being worked by other aircraft, the pilot is required to make contact with designated authority over or on the fire and receive permission to enter the fire traffic area and proceed with the mission or instructions to hold over a specified location. While the initial contact should be made approximately 12 miles out from the fire, it is good operating practice to monitor the assigned frequency and activity as far out as possible.

Drop priority is usually given to air tankers if they arrive over the fire at the same time as other aircraft. Smokejumper aircraft may be stacked on top of tankers. If the smokejumper aircraft is in the process of dropping jumpers, it will normally be allowed to continue until the personnel are all on the ground. At that time they may be asked to pull out of the area to allow the retardant aircraft to drop, returning to deliver the cargo after the air tanker is finished. If a jumper is injured in the drop, the jumper aircraft has priority over other aircraft to drop emergency supplies or provide other applicable assistance.

In some situations a combination of air activities can be accomplished safely on the same fire. This situation could occur when air tankers and helicopters are needed on opposite sides of the fire, traffic patterns can be flown well clear of the other activity and that good communication is maintained between all aircraft.

Proper radio procedures and discipline are very important in the fire environment. If you are unable to establish contact with the air attack, lead plane, or other aircraft over the incident, attempt contact on alternate frequencies or reconfirm the correct frequency with the applicable dispatch office. Air guard may be used to make initial contact and confirm working frequencies only as a last resort. It is primarily to be used as an emergency frequency. **No aircraft is to enter a fire traffic area without establishing radio contact with other aircraft working on the same fire.** Smokejumper aircraft being initial attack aircraft may be the first ones on secne and there will be no other aircraft.

5.2.1 FIRE TRAFFIC AREA DIAGRAM

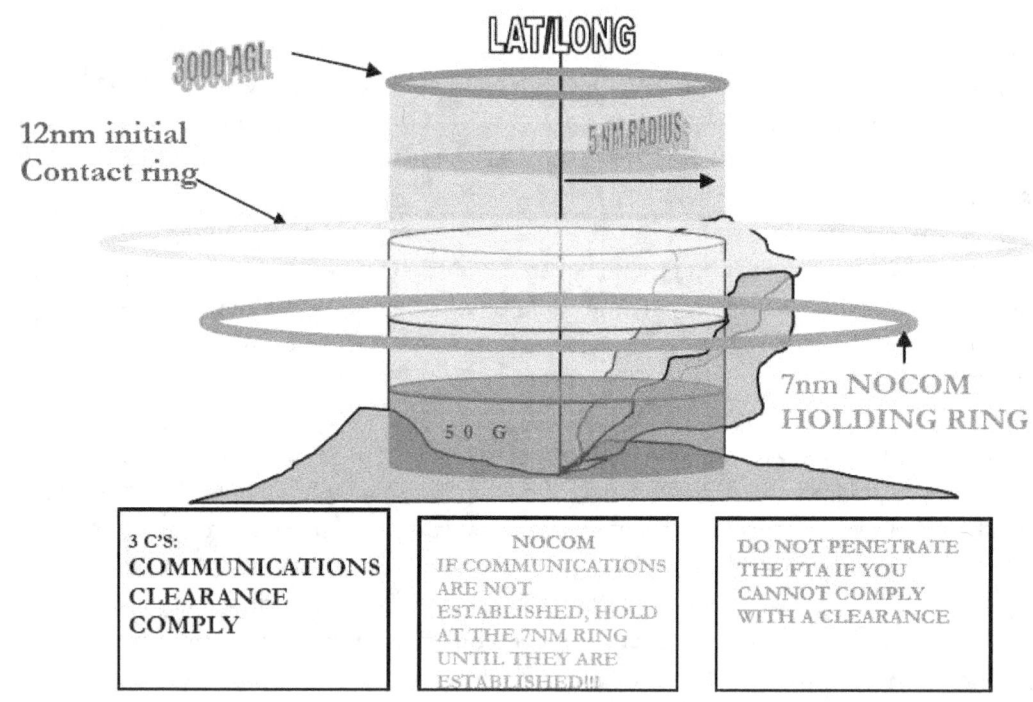

5.3 RESOURCE TRACKING AND FLIGHT FOLLOWING

All pilots flying aircraft under the administrative control of the USDA/USDI must notify the appropriate authorities of their intentions prior to initiating any flight. Filing flight plans (FAA or agency) , position reports, routing changes and records there of are intended to protect the welfare of crew and passengers in case of problems. Flight plans are also essential for efficient resource tracking and utilization. Common sense and consistent compliance with the following guidelines should minimize the possibilities of any aircraft being in difficulty for an extended period of time without proper follow up.

Most mission flights will be dispatched through the local or geographical area coordination centers, or with NICC (National Interagency Coordination Center, lower 48), which is involved in Interregional and Interagency movement of resources. Arrival notification and further instruction information will normally be relayed through the dispatch office in operation. If such a facility does not exist or is closed when the aircraft arrives, the pilot must make the call(s) necessary to close the flight plan with dispatch or NICC, let them know where he/she may be reached and when he/she will be legal to fly again. Check-ins to dispatch while enroute shall occur at designated intervals, depending upon mission and degree of risk. FAA IFR flight plans will be filed whenever appropriate, as well as FAA VFR flight plans for cross-country flights. Check-ins with Dispatch will be at 15 min intervals.

5.3.1 Automated Flight Following (AFF)

AFF is a satellite-based flight following system which exceeds agency minimum reporting intervals and offers safety and efficiency enhancements superior to radio flight following.

Automated Flight Following systems are authorized for use as a primary flight following method during BLM and USFS aviation operations as long as the AFF standards and requirements outlined in the National Mobilization Guide are met.

Resource Tracking and Flight Following:

> **Agency Flight Following** is done primarily for those flights taking place within a Geographic area. There are two types of Agency flight following: **Automated Flight Following (AFF), and Radio Check-in.** **AFF** is a satellite/web-based system. The dispatcher can "see" an aircraft icon on a computer screen and view, real time; it's location, speed, heading, altitude, and flight history. See 24.3.3 AFF procedures section, for more detailed information. **Radio Check-in / Check-out** flight following requires verbal communication via radio every 15 minutes. The dispatcher logs the aircraft call sign, location, and heading.
> *NOTE: An agreement between the pilot and dispatcher must be made on which type of Agency flight following will be utilized, preferably by phone prior to takeoff, but may be done via radio while airborne.*

Automated Flight Following (AFF) Procedures

> Automated Flight Following is one type of Agency flight following. Automated Flight Following reduces the requirement to "check in" via radio every 15 minutes, and provides

the dispatcher with a wide range of information on the flight, airspace, and other data that may be pertinent to the flight. This reduces pilot workload, clears overloaded radio frequencies, and provides the dispatcher with much greater detail and accuracy on aircraft location and flight history.

Requirements to Utilize Automated Flight Following:

- Procedures for flight requests, ordering aircraft, requirement for a Chief of Party, etc., are the same as radio check-in procedures.
- The aircraft must be equipped with the necessary hardware (transmitter and antenna).
- The dispatch office responsible for the flight following must have a computer connected to the Internet immediately available to them in the dispatch office. Dispatch office(s) responsible for flight following shall be staffed for the duration of the flight.
- Training: The flight following dispatcher must have a working knowledge of the automated flight following program (Webtracker) and must have a current username and password for the Automated Flight Following system.
- Automated Flight Following does **NOT** reduce or eliminate the requirement for aircraft on mission flights to have FM radio capability, and for the aircraft to be monitoring appropriate radio frequencies during the flight.
- When a flight will cross "boundaries" (example: A flight will originate on Unit A, fly on Unit A, then continue on to Units B and C) coordination between dispatch offices of Units A, B and C must be accomplished.

Procedures for Utilizing AFF :

1. When an aircraft is ordered, or a user requests flight following from a dispatch office, an agreement between the user and the dispatch office must be made that Automated Flight Following will be utilized.
2. Other standard information shall be communicated to the dispatch office, such as route of flight, passengers, purpose of flight, radio frequencies to monitor, known flight hazards, TFR information, ETD, etc. (no change from radio check-in procedures).
3. The dispatch office must log on to the Automated Flight Following web site, verify that the aircraft icon is visible on the screen, and be able to quickly monitor this page at any time during the flight.
4. If the flight will cross "traditional dispatch boundaries", the originating dispatch office must coordinate with affected units, and establish if the aircraft will be flight followed for the duration of the flight from the originating office or handed off when the border is crossed. Either option is acceptable but must be communicated and understood between dispatch offices and pilots/observers.
5. When aircraft is initially airborne, and outside of sterile cockpit environment, a radio call shall be made to the flight following dispatch office stating "Nxxxx off (airport or helibase name) AFF", dispatch office shall respond "Nxxxx, (dispatch call sign) AFF". This is required to positively verify that both the aircraft and the dispatch office are utilizing Automated Flight Following, radios are operational, and that the dispatcher can "see" the aircraft on the computer screen. If there is a problem at this point, revert to normal radio 15 minute check-in procedures until the problem is resolved.
6. The dispatch office then sets a 15 minute timer and, at a minimum, monitors the computer at 15 minute intervals for the duration of the flight.

7. When the aircraft has completed the flight and landed, the pilot or passenger (observer, Chief of Party, ATGS, etc.) shall contact the dispatch office via radio or telephone informing them that they are on the ground.

Procedures for Pilot/Observer:

1. Contact dispatch with request to utilize AFF (preferably via phone prior to flight).
2. Provide Dispatch with appropriate flight information (same as radio check-in procedures).
3. If Dispatch is willing and able to accommodate AFF request, obtain appropriate FM frequencies and tones to be monitored during flight and brief on radio calls you will make and what response is expected.
4. Shortly after take off, and outside of sterile cockpit environment, contact dispatch via radio stating "Nxxxx off (airport or helibase name) AFF".
5. If radio contact is not made with dispatch office, return to airport/helibase.
6. If radio contact is made, and AFF is verified by dispatch office, monitor assigned frequencies, including guard, for duration of flight.
7. If a deviation from planned and briefed flight route occurs, contact dispatch office via radio with the change.
8. If AFF capability is lost at the dispatch office, or the signal is lost during the flight, flight following will revert to 15 minute radio check-in procedures.
9. Monitor the appropriate radio frequencies at all times during the flight.
10. Inform dispatch upon landing that you are on the ground.

Procedures for Aircraft Dispatcher:

1. When AFF is requested, ensure AFF program access is available and request standard flight information from the pilot/Chief of Party (COP). Document using existing dispatch forms and logs.
2. Provide pilot/observer with appropriate frequencies to monitor during the flight (Dispatch frequency, National flight following, etc.). Ensure these frequencies are monitored during duration of flight.
3. If flight following will be handed off to another dispatch office during the flight, brief this with the pilot/COP, providing frequency change, call sign, and other appropriate information.
4. Brief with pilot/observer on radio calls expected and responses you will provide.
5. Check AFF system to ensure icon for the aircraft is shown.
6. Shortly after take off, pilot/COP will call via radio stating "Nxxxx off (airport or helibase name) AFF". Check aircraft icon color and verify time and date.
   Respond to the radio call, stating "Nxxxx, (dispatch call sign) AFF".
7. Keep the AFF system running on your computer during the entire flight.
8. Set 15 minute timer, and check flight progress as appropriate during the flight. Document using existing forms and logs.
9. If the icon turns RED, it means the signal has been lost. Immediately attempt contact with the aircraft via radio and follow normal lost communication, missing aircraft, or downed aircraft procedures as appropriate.
10. If radio contact is made after a lost signal, flight may continue utilizing 15 minute radio check-ins for flight following.
11. Use same procedure if computer system goes down during flight.

Hand Off Procedures for Dispatch Offices:

If a flight will cross "traditional dispatch boundaries", and the flight following will be handed off from one dispatch office to another, a positive hand off must be made. This must be coordinated between the affected dispatch offices and the aircraft, preferably prior to take off, but may be done while airborne. (Same as radio check-in procedures)

Coordination Requirements
Flight following hand offs must be coordinated when using AFF.

- Coordinate with affected dispatch offices and agree on who will be responsible for flight following, how it will be accomplished (AFF and/or radio check-ins), frequencies aircraft should monitor, and if frequency changes are required, when and where they should be made.
- Whenever possible utilize National Flight Following frequency (168.650) for entire flight.
- Ensure pilots/observers are briefed on any hand offs anticipated (call signs, frequencies and when to switch) and if a combination of AFF and radio check-ins will be required (when and where).

NOTE: Remember that Guard (168.625) is always available to make contact with an aircraft or dispatch office, and then move off guard to the appropriate frequency.

5.4 DOI OPERATED AIRCRAFT OPM2

Flight Plans. Pilots shall file and operate: a) on a Federal Aviation Administration (FAA) flight plan; or b) on an International Civil Aviation Organization (ICAO) flight plan; or c) in accordance with a bureau-approved flight plan program; or d) in accordance with an AMD Director approved vendor flight plan program specified in an AMD procurement document. Flight plans shall be filed prior to takeoff when possible.

Bureau flight plan programs may be used to accommodate specialized bureau missions and must be approved as delegated by the bureau Director. As a minimum, a bureau flight plan program must specify route of flight, estimated time of arrival (ETA), how an aircraft will be tracked during flight and response procedures should the aircraft experience a mishap or fail to check-in.

Flight Following. Pilots are responsible for flight following: a) with the FAA, or b) with the Appropriate ICAO entity, or c) in accordance with a bureau-approved flight following program, or d) in accordance with an AMD Director-approved vendor flight following program specified in an AMD procurement document. When communication is possible, position reporting shall not exceed one-hour intervals under normal circumstances.
Bureau flight following programs must be approved as delegated by the bureau Director. As a minimum, a bureau-approved flight following program must specify actions to be taken (e.g. notify the FAA) in the event of an overdue or missing aircraft. Position reports resulting from use of a bureau-approved flight following program must be documented by the receiving office and provide enough information to enable easy location of an overdue or missing aircraft.
An aircraft is considered "overdue" when it fails to arrive within 30-minutes past the ETA and cannot be located. An aircraft is considered "missing" when it has been reported to the FAA as being "overdue" and the FAA has completed an administrative search for the aircraft without success

Chapter

6

6.0 MOUNTAIN FLYING AND BACK COUNTRY AIRSTRIPS

6.1 INTRODUCTION

Flying missions in mountainous terrain requires special knowledge, experience and techniques to reduce the inherent risk of such operations. Rugged terrain, lack of suitable landing areas in the event of emergency, and adverse weather conditions add to the hazards involved.

6.2 DENSITY ALTITUDE

Aircraft operations at altitudes well above sea level and at higher than standard temperatures are commonplace in the western United States. Such operations always result in drastic reduction of airplane performance capabilities, because of the high density altitudes.
Density altitude is a measure of air density. It is not to be confused with pressure altitude, true altitude, or absolute altitude. It is not to be used as a height reference, but as determining criteria for the performance capability of an aircraft. Air density decreases with increase in altitude. As air density decreases, density altitude increases. The further effects of high temperature and high humidity are cumulative, resulting in an increasingly high density altitude condition. High density altitude reduces all aircraft performance parameters.
The means that normal horsepower output is reduced, propeller efficiency is reduced, and a higher true airspeed is required to sustain the airplane throughout its operating range. It means an increase in runway length requirements for takeoff and landing, and a decreased rate of climb. It should be noted that a turbo charged airplane provides some advantage in that it provides sea level horsepower up to a specified altitude above sea level.
Density altitude can be easily computed on most flight computers. Density altitude is pressure altitude corrected for nonstandard temperature. After computing density altitude, consult the manufacturer's performance data for your particular aircraft and do not operate outside the performance parameters.

6.3 MOUNTAIN WINDS

In the mountains, terrain interferes with the steady flow of air, which causes it to lift and sink in somewhat logical patterns. The shape of the terrain in its relation to the wind, the heating of slopes exposed to the sun, and steeply sloping ridges with jagged cuts (i.e. mountain passes), all cause predictable shifts in wind direction and speed. Moving air masses surge up and over terrain causing updraft on the upwind side of a ridge and sometimes extreme downdraft on the lee side as the air mass follows the terrain similar to the way water flows in a riverbed.

Terrain influence may cause the air to rise and descend again, taking on the aspect of a wave action for as far as 100 miles on the lee side of a mountain range.

Any abrupt change in angle between the terrain and wind flow can be expected to cause moderate to severe turbulence and wind shears that may be of such intensity that the structural integrity of the aircraft is jeopardized. Generally the strongest wind flow will be found at higher altitudes.

The heating of slopes causes thermal convection, with resultant lift over the source and downdraft as the thermal cools and disperses.

Mountain passes create a venturi effect as the air is forced through a smaller area and accelerated.

Ridge level winds in excess of 20 knots indicate that the pilot should proceed with caution. When they are 30 knots or more, consider staying on the ground or altering route of flight.

A mountain ridge line should be crossed at an angle to allow the pilot to turn away from the ridge with the least amount of turn required should down-drafts be encountered.

Winds aloft in the mountain West are predominantly westerly; however, surface winds may tend to flow up canyon from about noon until late in the evening, due to the unequal heating of the sunny slopes and shaded canyons.

Early morning and late evening flights will generally be less turbulent and can be made closer to the ridge line than during the heat of the day.

During reconnaissance flights in the heat of the day, special care should be taken near ridge tops and extra altitude should be used as needed. (See section on reconnaissance).

Always know where you are, where the nearest airstrip is, and how to reach the nearest terrain suitable for emergency landing.

Anticipate constantly changing winds. Do not rely on smoke drift or cloud shadows for surface wind direction. Never rely on riding an updraft to obtain sufficient altitude to clear the terrain. It could unexpectedly turn into a downdraft.

6.4 GENERAL

When flying up a narrow drainage, keep to one side so that you may observe any emergency landing sites in the bottom of the canyon, safely complete a 180 degree turn for an emergency exit, and take advantage of rising air on the upwind side of the canyon.

Generally fly down drainage. When flying up drainage, ALWAYS rate the topography ahead and maintain proper position and sufficient altitude to turn around. The grade of the canyon may climb faster than you can.

Use caution when operating in the vicinity of rainsqualls and low stratus clouds. Never go into any type of cloud while flying at low altitude in the mountains. If IFR is inevitable, a precautionary landing should be seriously considered, even if it may result in damage to the aircraft.

Proper flight following is extremely important. If you go down it may be a long time before help arrives due to the size of the wilderness.

Do not be lulled into complacency by a weather report giving the ceiling at 1500 to 2000 feet. Mountains may surround the reporting station 2000 to 5000 feet higher than the station. Insist on visibility as well as ceiling when flying in mountainous areas. Snow and rain can quickly reduce forward visibility to zero. Darkness often blends in perfectly with the color of the mountain, which may appear to be just another dark section of the sky.

Be familiar with the destination airport. In advance of the flight, review available charts for altitude, length of runway, and obstructions.

Remember that spotting landmarks may be difficult; a mountain shown as 8000 to 9000 feet on the charts may appear as a small knoll if the peak rises out of surrounding terrain having an elevation of 4000 or 5000 feet.

Always be on the lookout for wires and cables across canyons.

Don't operate into or out of high mountain areas with a tight schedule. Give yourself plenty of time; weather must take precedence over any schedule.

Fly equipped with an emergency survival kit. In the event of a forced landing, the general rule is to stay with the airplane.

6. 5 BACK COUNTRY AIRSTRIPS

1. General.

Pilots must have a current mountain airstrip sign-off on their pilot cards prior to operating on backcountry airstrips. Most of these airstrips are located in central Idaho and the Selway-Bitteroot area of Montana.

Qualified flight crews may be involved in pickup and delivery of personnel and equipment from marginal airstrips located in rugged terrain. These operations can, at times, be classed as hazardous, depending on the capability of the airplane, atmospheric conditions, and condition of the airstrip. The surface of these strips usually is sand, sod, or gravel, or a combination of all three. Pilots should carefully check usage requirements for all strips prior to planning a stop. Some are privately owned, with public use reserved for emergencies. Others are open only when using the resort facilities. Almost all strips can be used for fire-related activity, but this must be arranged through dispatch.

For the most part, USFS/BLM maintains or has access to a "current condition" status of all airfields within their area of coverage and will not dispatch an aircraft there unless the airfield is reported to be in good condition. It is also standard practice to stand down on most of these airfields during periods of hot, gusty and turbulent air conditions—normally between 1000 and 1800 hours during the summer.

Each airfield has its own peculiarity and on the marginal strips pilots should be thoroughly checked out before being approved for or accepting a mission. Many strips are laid out, by necessity, in terrain where there is only one way in and one way out. Very few have been constructed on completely level ground and many have a series of humps, swells, and side slopes. They are often unattended; therefore, hazards such as wild or domestic animals, washouts, and overgrowth may be encountered. Know your airplane and understand its capabilities and limitations, as well as your own. Make every effort to maintain your proficiency in short field techniques and slow flight. Plan trips in the early morning whenever possible. Air instability begins around 1000 and grows worse until evening. Keep your airplane as light as possible. Carry only what you know will permit a safe operation. Know the field you are going into—the length, temperature, and hazards. Check field conditions with other pilots when possible. Many of these fields have one-way approaches with no go-around.

2. Approach

Look the strip over thoroughly before you commit to a landing. There may be some obstructions that were not present before, if necessary, conduct a low-level drag of the airstrip before landing, terrain permitting. Keep a sharp lookout for other traffic both in the air and on the field. To meet another aircraft taking off in the opposite direction while you are coming down the canyon "slow and dirty" could be disastrous, Announce intentions on 122.9 or other appropriate frequency.Plan your approach carefully. In some cases, terrain will hide the field until you are on short final. Look both the approach and departure over while you are at a safe altitude. If you feel doubtful about the approach, go around while you are still high. DO NOT commit yourself to an approach until you feel comfortable with its parameters. Many approaches do not allow a go around after final.

Use a stabilized power approach whenever possible. Low, slow approaches leave you behind the power curve and at the mercy of downdrafts. The minimum airspeed for a power approach is approximately 1.3 times Vso plus 50 percent of the gust factor. Higher speed (1.5 Vso) should be used in the event of a power off approach, Although use of full flaps is normally recommended for routine landings, the drag could overcome the power available at high-density altitudes, making go arounds difficult or impossible. This should be kept in mind during approaches to back country airstrips, particularly in the "low, slow" environment. If wind conditions are causing gusts, wind shifts, or whirlwinds (dust devils), the approach and landing should not be made. These winds can be turbulent, shearing, and put the aircraft out of control.

3. Landing

Fly throughout the approach and landing with controlled airspeed and pitch. Most backcountry pilots agree that pitch primarily controls airspeed and power primarily controls altitude during visual approaches to back country airstrips.

Plan the touchdown as near the approach end of the runway as practical for that given airstrip, giving consideration to slope and moving air surrounding terrain features, and keeping in mind that downdrafts may be present.

Give particular attention to drift correction and directional control after landing.

Proper use of controls during the landing roll is very important. Crosswind should not generally be a concern during backcountry operations because much wind is not acceptable for operations. However, slope, side slope, and surface conditions may very much be of concern. Maintain directional control using whatever control deflection and power is necessary.

If braking is desired, raising the flaps immediately after touchdown will increase the effectiveness. In turboprop aircraft, beta and reverse will generally be much more effective than wheel braking.

Use caution when taxiing off the runway. There may be holes, rocks, or other hazards under the grass. If in doubt, stop and walk the area first. Move the airplane off the runway for parking. The next person to land may need the entire runway available.

Take care to keep animals away from the airplane. Cattle and horses like to scratch themselves by rubbing against wing struts and other surfaces. Dogs often find whirling propellers fascinating.

4. Takeoff

The mountain runway environment requires a thorough pre-flight analysis and careful consideration of at least the following for takeoff:

Analyze the takeoff conditions carefully. If the air is bad or a tail wind is blowing, WAIT IT OUT. Don't load more weight than you are sure the airplane can handle. If you have any doubt, split the load and arrange to pick it up later. Is the runway long enough, or is the slope prohibitive? A 1 percent down slope is generally equivalent to 10 percent more runway and generally takes precedence over wind direction in deciding which way to go. If the surface is sod, is it stable, spongy, or rough? Early spring thaws or rains may result in unstable, slick, or sticky surface conditions.

Use the proper short/, soft field technique for the particular aircraft. Either pulling the aircraft off early or leaving it on the ground too long can significantly decrease performance.

Wind conditions are critical. Are the wind conditions within the capabilities of both the airplane and pilot? Strong downdrafts and wind shear encountered at lift-off are very critical.

What is the density altitude and how is it going to affect the performance of the airplane? Can a lower gross weight compensate for the loss of performances, Is it necessary to wait for more favorable conditions regarding density altitude and/or wind?

The pilot, having considered these factors in the decision to go, should observe the manufactures recommendation regarding the use of flaps. On takeoff, accelerate the airplane smoothly, rotating to the pitch attitude at which it will lift off and fly, using full power and best mixture for the density altitude.

5. Climb out

Once the aircraft is airborne, can it stay airborne and clear the intervening obstructions? Can it out climb the surrounding terrain?

When airborne, a pitch attitude should be established that will produce Vx until obstacles are cleared, then Vy. As altitude increases, Vx and Vy converge until they meet at the service ceiling. Most experienced mountain pilots consider airspeed more important than altitude after liftoff, and will obtain extra airspeed for marginal wind conditions.

During the climb out, the use of precise airspeed, attitude, and power control is essential, and any inclination to be influenced by the false horizon effect of local terrain must be avoided. The pilot should attempt to fly in areas of possible or observed lift, and be alert to the position of the sun and its possible blinding effect during lift off and climb out. In piston aircraft it may be necessary to level off during climb-out to prevent engine overheat.

Chapter

7

7.0 Low Level Operations

7.1 LOW LEVEL OPERATIONS

7.1.1 OBJECTIVES

The objectives are to outline proficiency requirement and operational recommendations for the BLM and USFS low level flight operations. To promote operational safety the following guidelines for low level operations and pilot proficiency requirements have been established.

7.1.2 DEFINITIONS

Low level operations: Any planned flight at less than 500 feet from the surface. (Not including takeoff or landing or Enroute weather considerations).

Personal Protective Equipment (PPE): Flash fire protection, and the Occupational Safety and Health Administration (OSHA) requirements for hearing conservation and eye protection. Flight crews and passengers engaged in special use activities are required to wear the appropriate aviation life support equipment.

Special Use Activities: Operations involving the utilization of airplanes and helicopters in support of Agency programs which are not point-to-point flight activities and which require special considerations due to their functional use. Special pilot qualifications and techniques, special aircraft equipment, and PPE are required to enhance the safe transportation of personnel and property.

7.1.3 REGULATIONS

14 CFR Part 91.3	Responsibility and authority of the pilot in command.
14 CFR Part 91.13	Careless or reckless operation.
14 CFR Part 91.15	Dropping objects.
14 CFR Part 91.119	Minimum safe altitudes: General.
14 CFR Part 135.117	Passenger briefing.

7.1.4 DEVIATIONS AND WAIVERS/EXEMPTIONS

Deviations: Life-threatening emergencies may require deviation from Departmental Manual, Federal Aviation Regulations, and Forest Service policy. For in-flight emergencies, the pilot shall take appropriate action to assure safety of flight. Deviations shall be reported as soon as possible to the appropriate authority and documented on a SAFECOM.

Waivers/Exemptions: The Department of the Interior and USFS has obtained low level waivers from the Department of Transportation, FAA. The waivers are specific in nature and should be reviewed prior to operational use. There is no Service-wide waiver or exemption. To review current waivers and exemptions for your agency go to http://aes.faa.gov or your agencies directives.

7.1.5 LOW LEVEL OPERATIONS REQUIREMENTS

Pilot Qualifications and Experience: A pilot shall meet the requirements as outlined in 351 DM 3.2B or FSM 5700. Vendor PIC qualifications are listed in 350 DM 3.3A., FSM 5700 and this document In addition to the basic pilot qualifications the pilot must have 200 hours PIC in category, in low level operations (agriculture applications, power/pipeline patrol, refuge survey, game counting, where extended operations below 500 feet AGL are conducted. Operations that do not qualify are traffic watch, banner towing, aerial photography, and flight instruction).

Aircraft Requirements: Only aircraft that have been carded by AMD specifically for low level operations may be used. The aircraft must have a strobe light visible from above, fire extinguisher, first aid kit, and survival kit.

Carrying Passengers: Only designated observers and flight crew members, who have been trained and designated as necessary to the mission may be carried during low level operations.

Personal Protective Equipment: All personnel on board aircraft participating in low level operations shall wear PPE:
1. Fire resistant clothing (Nomex flight suit).
   2 All-leather, or leather and Nomex gloves.
   3. Leather boots, above the ankle. (ALSE Handbook Page 4 paragraph E) DOI only.

Observer/Air crewmember Briefing: The observers/air crewmembers will be briefed before the first takeoff of the day by the PIC in accordance with 14 CFR 135.

Mission Briefing: The observer/crew member will brief the PIC on the mission. Discussion will follow as to expected route, potential hazards, and expected responsibilities of the observer/crew member during the flight and during an emergency.

Regulations: 14 CFR Part 91.119 states that airplanes cannot operate closer than 500 feet to any person, vessel, vehicle, or structure. This regulation must be followed, unless specifically exempted by the FAA.

Grants of exemptions: The United States Forest Service and the Department of the Interior both have grants of exemptions for operations in congested areas. Please review them for the most current information available. http://aes.faa.gov

7.1.6 LOW LEVEL RECOMMENDED PROCEDURES AND

TECHNIQUES FOR AIRPLANES

Aircraft Maneuvering and Configuration: The observer can usually get a good look at the area of interest by flying in a comfortable slow-flight@ speed (1.3 Vso) and one notch of flaps or the manufacture's recommended settings, remembering stall speed increases with angle of bank.

1. Pilots should review and be proficient in slow flight and around pylon type maneuvers.

A. Optimum pivotal altitude above the ground, angle of bank, and lateral distance from the target area must be considered while keeping the observer in proper position throughout the turn, being sure not to block the target with the wing.

B. The pilot should plan the approach path carefully having the airspeed, altitude, and attitude stabilized prior to arrival over the observation point. Dive bomber type approaches should be avoided.

C. If a return to the target is required after a low pass, a climb of at least 200 feet should be made prior to making the turn back to the target if necessary enter a racetrack type pattern.

Terrain: Pilots should not fly an extended observation track up-slope or into a box canyon where the aircraft would be unable to turn around. Escape routes should always be considered, turning away and down from rising terrain.

Wind and Weather Considerations: Upwind low level observation passes should be made whenever possible. An extra margin of airspeed should be carried in downwind situations. Avoid operations close to terrain when windy conditions exist. During adverse wind and weather conditions a stop to the flight should be considered opting for more favorable conditions.

Flight Hazards: While conducting low level operations the following hazards should be considered:

1. Structures. Man-made structures such as power or communication lines, and towers requires careful consideration, especially when flying near canyons, rivers, and over unfamiliar terrain. When possible a high level pass or reconnaissance should be made of the area noting potential hazards for future reference. The pilot and observer should work as a team. Even more than normal the pilot should concentrate on piloting duties and allow the observer to make the observations.
2. Birds. Pilots should avoid birds whenever possible but violent evasive maneuvers should not be taken. Birds will usually dive from the aircraft flight path but a bird strike is much less eventful than a stall at low level.
3. Density altitude. When operating at medium and high elevations on hot days can decrease the aircraft of performance. Pilots should refer to the aircraft performance charts and carry an extra margin when operating in high density altitudes.
4. Lighting. The lighting is a consideration when working around water or a low sun condition. While observing the sun should be kept behind or to the non-target side to avoid sun blinding.
5. Flat turns. Flat turns should only be used when following terrain or rivers to assist the observer, but should not be considered during turns. Climbing, coordinated turns are to be made when changing direction or circling a target.

Chapter

8.0 TRAINING AND EVALUATION

8.1 PIC / SIC / INSTRUCTOR / INSPECTOR REQUIRMENTS

PIC	Instructor	Inspector-Checkairman	Additional
Annual Ground School	In addition to PIC requirements to the left.	In Addition to PIC and Instructor requirements to the left. (Excluding 100 hours make and model).	
Annual Equipment Check Ride	Qualified aircraft instructors are eligible to be Designated by the respective National Office as IOE Captains.	Designation by National F/W Standardization Officer or Aviation Management Directorate (*). All Checkairman/Inspectors will meet the requirements of the ISPOG.	*BLM National Aviation Office concurrence with AMD for Bureau Pilots.
Annual Smokejumper PIC Checkride / Card issued and signed.			
6-Month IFR Check Ride	CFI, CFII, MEI	1 Year Active Smokejumper Pilot Instructor.	
		Instructor Qualification for 2 Years.	
Annual Autopilot Endorsement (if installed).	Standardization Check Ride and National Office designation.	Standardization Check Ride for both the BLM and USFS by the Flight Standards Pilot.	
Annual Line Check	100 Hours in Make and Model	Multi-regional Experience	
Initial Operating Experience (IOE) 25 Hours in Make and Model. **		3 Years Smokejumper Pilot Experience	** See PIC note # 3 on page 49
	SIC- Annual Equipment Check Ride for SIC		
Aircraft Commander Evaluation Board for First Type Rating.	Initial - 5 Practice jumps as SIC.	100 Missions	
Biennial Standardization Workshop (USFS).	Recurrent - 1 refresher flight with paracargo	Current and mission qualified.	
Biennial Qualification Review (USFS)	Meet Far 135.245 and FAR 121 Appendixes F.	Smokejumper Inspector Pilot Biennial Standardization Workshop and Check Ride.	

8.2 ADVANCED SMOKEJUMPER OPERATIONS

Smokejumper Pilot - Syllabus

Text:

Interagency Smokejumper Pilots Operations Guide

Departmental Manual (BLM)

FSM 5700 (USFS)

Aircraft specific Flight Manual.

Spotter Training Manual (USFS or BLM)

Video:

Professional Smokejumper Pilot Video

Smokejumper Spotter Video

Description:

This course is designed as a structured and standardized training program of ground and flight training for both agency and contract smokejumper pilot candidates.

Goals:

1. To become an integral part of a crew that safely delivers smokejumpers by either the BLM or USFS parachute delivery systems and subsequently delivers paracargo at low levels in support of that or other missions.
2. Safely plan and perform smokejumper missions.
3. Safely plan and perform paracargo missions
4. Standardize smokejumper pilot training and operations
5. Receive an Interagency smokejumper captain's card.

Requirements:

Annual Ground School
Annual Equipment Check Ride
6-Month IFR Check Ride
Initial Operating Experience (IOE)
25 Hours in Make and Model

Evaluation:

Designated check airman

Phase Training:

Each phase of the training syllabus may encompass multiple ground and flight sessions.

8.2.1   PHASE 1

The program calls for a smokejumper instructor pilot (IP) and a spotter to work as a team in training the pilot candidate. Optimally, the same IP and spotter should work with the candidate throughout the course of the program.

Primarily, the spotter: does spot determinations, patterns, and altitudes pertaining to equipment used. Primarily, the IP: monitors power, configuration, airspeed, altitude, attitude, safety, and cargo patterns and drops.

Each ground training session will be conducted by the IP and the Spotter and will include an in depth briefing of the upcoming flight. The objectives for each lesson will be clearly defined and discussed with the candidate.

8.2.2 Phase 1 Ground - Introduction to Basic Smokejumper Operations

I: Phase 1 Indoctrination:
  a. Professional Smokejumper Pilot video
  b. Professional Smokejumper Spotter video

II: Smokejumper mission
  a. Initial attack, varied duties
  b. Additional jobs - resupply, heavy cargo, back country retrieval
  c. High training standards for jumpers and pilots
  d. Safety standards and concerns regarding the mission

III: Smokejumper equipment
  a. Tour of the loft
  b. Basic smokejumper equipment
      1. Jump gear and parachute—rounds and squares
      2. Fire packs
      3. Cubies
      4. Saws
      5. Spurs
      6. Radios
  c. Cargo delivery system
      1. High and low impact
      2. Different size chutes

IV: Spotting

     a. What is a spotter - expertise required

     b. Spotter responsibilities—picking the spot, etc.

     c. Pilot/spotter relationship

V: Operational Procedures

     a. Jump ship patterns (standard and downwind, crosswind, turns and banks)

          1. Corrections (standard/non-standard)

          2. Pattern call-outs

     b. Streamer patterns

          1. Determining jump spot, pattern direction

          2. Initial, standard, crosswind, downwind

          3. Altitude/airspeed

          4. Streamers away

          5. Streamer visibility - spotter and pilot

          6. Selecting exit point

          7. Streamer check set—why

          8. Check set final (i.e., streamers to spot)

          9. Common errors

     c. Jumper drop pattern

          1. Altitude/airspeed/flap settings/power application   (rounds and squares)

          2. When and how to abort

          3. Pilot to spotter communication of conditions

          4. Jumpers away

          5. Climb to 3000, AGL for ram airs

     d. Cargo

          1. DZ selection

          2. Altitude/airspeed

          3. Dry run

          4. Calls

          5. Lead/drift

          6. Commands - "on final, standby, kick "

          7. Aborting cargo run - why, call-outs

          8. Accuracy - communication with ground and kicker

          9. Accuracy is always sacrificed for safety

     e. Emergency Procedures

8.2.3 Phase 1 Flight - Basic Smokejumper Mission Flight Procedures

Objective: To introduce the pilot candidate to the basic mission flight maneuvers and operational procedures and to develop the skills necessary to effectively accomplish these.

The IP will be in the right seat, spotter in the door. The initial lesson is conducted over flat, open terrain with easily identified spots. The candidate should be able to fly streamer observation and jump patterns from any direction without having to concentrate on terrain avoidance at this point. Emphasis should be on understanding the purpose of each maneuver, a clear understanding of what the spotter requires to do his job, clear and concise communication and good operational coordination with the spotter. Emphasize smooth, coordinated maneuvering and consistent altitude, airspeed and heading control.

I. Straight flight along a road, power line, etc.

    a. Left and right corrections on spotter's call standard 5 degree, non standard whatever the spotter calls for.

Turns will be smooth and coordinated, no rudder turns. Watch for a tendency to drift back to the original line after a correction is made. Don't let the candidate rely exclusively on the DG or heading bug to hold their line. Have them make use of ground reference points and a point on the horizon.

II. Streamer patterns

    a. Proper positioning on observation pattern

        1. Keeping spotter in position

        2. Pilot observation of streamers to the ground (where to look)

        3. Streamers to spot

Bank angle should not exceed 30 degrees. Monitor airspeed and altitude control. Good communication with the spotter is important. Streamer to spot to exit point line should use ground reference points to hold the line. Emphasize pilot awareness of exit point.

III. Jump patterns

    a. Consistent line on final

    b. Proper size pattern

    c. Proper altitude and airspeed

*The candidate should be using ground and horizon reference points to turn on line and maintain it along with the directional gyro. Altitude and airspeed control is crucial along with power management at jumper exit. Turn off final should not be made until "jumpers away" call.

IV. Cargo dropping

    a. Drop zone selection

        1. Communication with spotter regarding DZ - may need to be different from jump spot. Type of cargo and chute size.

        2. Good entry and exit routes

        3. Down canyon and down sun

        4. Lead in points

        5. Dry run

6. Commands
7. Lead/drift for accuracy
8. Aborting a live run
9. Safety
10. Aircraft configuration: Flaps and Power settings, airspeed control, clean up during exit

8.2.4 Phase 2 ground - Advanced Smokejumper Operations

I. Observation pass
    a. Low pass at spotters option
        1. No pass lower than 200' AGL
    b. Why the spotter would request a low pass

II. Jump spot selection
    a. Hazards and terrain considerations in selecting a spot and a jump pattern
    b. Alternate spots

III. Jump altitude
    a. Minimum altitude and why—rounds vs. squares ("on final 3000 or 1500')
    b. Jump altitude is over the exit point not the jump spot
    c. Determining altitude
        1. Timing streamers
        2. Radar altimeter
        3. Low pass

IV. Determining wind drift/velocity
    a. Accurate release of streamers over jump spot - why?
    b. Selecting exit point
    c. Terrain factors
        1. Needs to see streamers all the way to the ground to determine wind line
        2. Understand the spotters' counting method to exit point (effected by wind speed and the need to determine the exit point) and the importance of maintaining the airspeed you will use on the jumprun. The Wind cone concept and parachute performance parameters - spotter.

V. Jump patterns
    a. Non-standard patterns
        1. Downwind pattern terrain and ground speed considerations
        2. Crosswind pattern - same
        3. Right hand patterns
        4. Spotter guiding pilot onto proper pattern
    b. Changing line on final
        1. Offsetting the line left or right to parallel original line
        2. Pivoting the line left or right with the jump spot as pivot point (clock method).

    c. Emergencies
        1. Critical (Mass exit, Jumper in tow—spotter/pilot comm.)
        2. Non-critical

VI. Cargo dropping
    a. DZ selection - terrain factors
        1. Ridge top
        2. Side hill
        3. Canyon bottom
    b. Considerations with different bundle weights and chute size
        1. Free fall delivery
        2. High altitude dropping
    c. Variations with different kickers
        1. Pilot makes corrections not the kicker
    d. Importance of smooth maneuvering
        1. Impact of steep turns and high "G", maneuvers and pull outs on cargo kickers
            in the back of the airplane

8.2.5 Phase 2 Flight- Advanced Smokejumper Mission Flight Procedures

Objective: To develop the pilot candidates' skills to the operational level by introducing successively more difficult, steep terrain for jump spots and cargo DZs, non-standard patterns and emergency procedures. Candidate will be able to work effectively and efficiently with the spotter in streamer observation patterns and jump patterns. Cargo dropping will emphasize safety and planing ahead for emergencies in the more difficult terrain. Emphasis will be on situational awareness in typical terrain and technical skills needed to fly the smokejumper mission in mountainous terrain. Smooth, coordinated maneuvering and maintaining correct airspeed, altitude and heading should be developed at this level to where the IP has little need to point out corrections.

I. Observation pass
    a. Low pass at no less than 200' AGL
        1. Put spotter in proper position to see jump spot
        2. Communicate pilot observation of atmospheric conditions - wind, turbulence,
            up and down drafts

II. Streamer patterns
    a. Proper observation pattern
    b. Throwing check streamers for non standard patterns downwind and crosswind
        1. Good communication between spotter and pilot of pattern changes

III. Jump patterns
    a. Standard and non-standard
    b. Spotter changing final line
    c. Terrain factors
    d. Emergency procedures

IV. Cargo dropping
>   a. Recon and dry run
>   b. Planning entry and exit routes with emergencies in mind
>   c. Changing pattern for safety and accuracy
>   d. Smooth flying - no hard turns of "G" loading on pull out if possible
>   e. Emergencies procedures
>   f. Test standard for accuracy

Spotter will set up successively more difficult jump scenarios. Spotter will set up jump pattern and corrections, but the pilot candidate will recon the cargo DZ (both on the jump spot and at an alternate spot) and set up the cargo run. Emphasize safety and good judgement in all phases, especially on selecting and flying cargo runs.

8.2.6 Phase 3 Ground - Smokejumper Mission Topics

I. Pilot and spotter responsibilities
a. Flight and jumper safety

II. Radio communications
a. Pilot to spotter system in the aircraft
b. VHF and FM communications - who is responsible for what
c. Current frequency lists

III. Flight planning
>   a. Navigation - familiarity with long range navigation equipment
>   b. Fuel-jumper load with required reserve
>   c. Check NOTAMS, TFRs and Hazards maps

IV. Standby and Dispatch
>   a. Daily base operations, including pilot/spotter briefings.
>   b. Dispatch procedure - check-ins
>   c. Duty limits, flight time limits, mandatory days off
>   d. PPE - nomex
>   e. Agency regulations, forms and paperwork
>   f. Loadmaster/Flight Attendant role

V. Other missions
>   a. Crew hauls
>   b. Paracargo
>   c. Jumper retrieval
>   d. Point to Point cargo

VI. Practice jumps

VII. Fire Protocol
   a. Air Attack roles
   b. Mission priority
   c. Radio communications/ dispatch and required checkins
   d. Multiple aircraft on site
   e. Lights
   f. Fire Traffic Area (FTA)

8.2.7 Phase 3 Flight - Prep For Checkride and Live Cargo Drops

This phase will prepare the candidate for the final checkride with an agency inspector. The spotter will simulate a real jump request.The candidate will be familiar with aircraft performance charts and be able to determine if mission can be accomplished under conditions of the simulation. IP input and corrections should be minimal at this point.

I.   Observation pass, streamer passes

II. Jump run

III. Cargo run

IV. Simulated emergencies (deploying jumpers after takeoff, engine loss with jumpers and on cargo runs, cargo hung up, etc.) Potential emergency situations requiring smokejumper bailout are varied and detailed procedures for every conceivable situation are not possible. General bailout procedures for non-critical situations (such as landing gear malfunction) and critical emergencies (such as engine failure due to contaminated fuel) will be discussed in classroom training. Smokejumper spotters are trained to respond to all emergency situations with the command to the jumpers of "stay put", . Appropriate action then gets started with the spotter in control and the pilot free of aft CG problems.

The candidate should be able to perform all operations to mission ready standards. Live cargo drops should be practiced for accuracy. Live drops can be in an area where cargo retrieval will be fairly easy.

8.2.8 The Checkride

This guide is the evaluation standard for smokejumper/paracargo checkrides. The proper agency form in Chapter 10 will be used by the check pilot. The candidate will be required to take either a written or oral exam based on this guide and calculate a smokejumper related weight and balance. Should the check airman elect to conduct in-flight simulated emergencies during special use missions, engine failures shall only be simulated by retarding a power lever or throttle. Mission oriented emergencies will be preplanned with the spotter.

Chapter 9

9.0 FLIGHT CREW QUALIFICATIONS

9.1 MINIMUM QUALIFICATIONS

Large Aircraft Captains must have a minimum of the following:

9.1.2 ALL AIRCRAFT (AGENCY PILOTS)

1. FAA ATP Pilot Certificate

2. Current FAA Medical Certificate appropriate to category/class

3. Type rating for appropriate aircraft

4. 1500 Total time

5. 1200 PIC in airplanes

6. 500 PIC category and class to be flown

7. 200 PIC in typical terrain

8. 100 PIC in category preceding 12 months

9. 100 Night

10. 50 Instrument in flight

11. 75 Instrument actual/simulated

12. 10 PIC in category preceding 60 days

13. 25 PIC make and model or type within 5 years

14. 100 PIC turbine

15. 10 PIC make and model preceding 12 months

16. Pilot qualification card with proper sign off

17. **250 hours PIC in aircraft over 12,500 pounds maximum gross weight (DOI)**

9.2. LARGE AIRCRAFT

1. Agency Pilots: Complete upgrade per Aircraft Commander Evaluation Board found in the 5709.16 (USFS) and the BLM Aviation Standard Operations Procedures.

2. Contract Pilots must meet the requirements under their respective agencies (DOI/USFS) contract specifications.

3. After receiving an initial Type Rating and successful completion of IOE pilots will be designated PIC Point to Point only.

4. All agency pilots, *regardless* of the mission must complete the Large Aircraft Evaluation Board to become Large Aircraft Commander qualified.

9.2.1 AIRCRAFT COMMANDER EVALUATION BOARD

The purpose of this board is to approve candidates for upgrade to aircraft commander in airplanes with a gross takeoff weight above 12,500 pounds or that require a type rating. This position will hereinafter be referred to as large aircraft commander. The intention is to base the upgrade to large aircraft commander on performance and experience rather than minimum flight hour criteria.

The board will be will consist of five members representing the USFS, BLM and AMD. Board members will be appointed by the respective agencies and will be agency captains with check airman authority and a depth of experience in both operations and management. The board will designate additional captains as a standing cadre to serve as evaluators when requested by the board. Members are identified by letter annually or upon change of membership. Board membership will be comprised of the U.S.F.S. National Fixed Wing Standardization Pilot, the U.S.F.S. National Smokejumper Program Manager, the BLM Flight Standards / Transport Category Pilot, the AMD Fixed Wing Specialist and a U.S.F.S. Regional representative. The board will meet annually and additional meetings may be held when deemed necessary by the board.

The OPM ~~Operating Manual for Qualification Standards for General Schedule Positions~~ (p. IV-B-282) for Aircraft Operation Series states:

"Minimum eligibility requirements for positions in the occupation are based on 1) possession of the appropriate Federal Aviation Administration (FAA) pilot certificates and/or appropriate military ratings, 2) meeting the applicable flight hour requirements, and 3) possession of the knowledge and skills required for the positions."

In order to meet the letter and intent of the three conditions outlined in the statement above, all USFS and DOI large aircraft commanders must meet the following minimum requirements.

9.2.2 FLIGHT CREW QUALIFICATIONS

1. A current FAA ATP pilot certificate with appropriate type rating.

2. The following flight hours:
   - 1500 hours Total Time
   - 1200 hours Pilot in Command
   - 500 hours Multi-engine
     - 250 hours multi-engine PIC experience
     - 100 hours heavy multi-engine experience (PIC or SIC) **USFS only.**
     - 250 hours heavy multi-engine PIC experience, **DOI only.**
   - 75 hours Instrument – actual or simulated
   - 50 hours Instrument – in flight
   - 100 hours Night
   - 100 hours Turbine Engine Experience (PIC or SIC)

3. Possession of the required knowledge and skills as evidenced by a designation as aircraft commander from the Aircraft Commander Evaluation Board.

All agency pilots who will be flying as a large aircraft commander, whether new hire or upgrade will go through the board evaluation and designation. If the candidate's large multi-engine airplane experience is in excess of 250 hours as pilot in command, the board may elect to reduce the number of evaluation flights based on performance. If the candidate is a DOI employee, this evaluation process may also serve as the initial flight evaluation required by 351 DM 3.4.

It should be noted that this process is intended to evaluate the candidate's potential as an aircraft commander and is not concerned with a specific mission qualification. This does not apply solely to smokejumper pilot candidates.

For the purposes of this document the following definitions will apply:

- **Pilot in Command experience** – that flight time logged as defined in FAR Part 1: Definitions and Abbreviations,
  - Pilot in command means the person who:
    - Has the final authority and responsibility for the operation and safety of flight;
    - Has been designated as pilot in command before or during the flight; and
    - Holds the appropriate category, class, and type rating, if appropriate, for the conduct of the flight.

- **Large Aircraft** – aircraft of more than 12,500 pounds maximum certificated takeoff weight, or requires a type rating to be pilot in command.

Candidates wishing to be considered for upgrade to aircraft commander will submit a recommendation package to the board. The candidate will be type rated prior to the package being submitted. The recommendation package will consist of a written recommendation for upgrade from the candidate's supervisor, training records (including type training), and flight experience records and upgrade recommendations from line captains who have flown with the candidate.

If the candidate is already qualified as a large aircraft commander and this is an additional aircraft to be added to their designation as aircraft commander, the candidate need only submit the upgrade recommendation and the type certificate training records. In this case the board, at their discretion, may approve the additional qualification with no evaluation flights.

If the initial package review is satisfactory, the board will recommend the candidate for evaluation flights. Based on the candidates experience a plan of action will be developed by the board for each evaluation flight. This will insure that any concerns and or issues board members may have with the applicant will be addressed during the appropriate evaluation flight.

The board may elect to designate the candidate as an aircraft commander with less than three evaluation flights. It should be noted that these are *evaluation* flights, not *checkrides*.

- **Evaluation Flight 1** – This flight is intended to establish the candidate's general level of proficiency in the aircraft, CRM and ability to command the aircraft and crew. If the candidate satisfactorily completes this flight they will be recommended for Evaluation Flight 2.
- **Evaluation Flight 2** – This evaluation may consist of multiple flights and will include actual and/or simulated IFR and Enroute scenarios, aerial fire fighting missions (if appropriate) and back country flight/airport operations (if appropriate). Satisfactory completion will result in recommendation for Evaluation Flight 3.
- **Evaluation Flight 3** – Satisfactory completion of this flight will result in USFS candidates being signed off as aircraft commander and DOI candidates being recommended for their agency qualification check ride.

If mission training has been completed prior to the evaluation flights, Evaluation Flight 2 or 3 can be a mission qualification check ride with concurrence of the board members.

A different board member will conduct each Evaluation Flight. All evaluations will be documented in detail and any deficiencies in skill or judgment will be clearly identified. Remedial training at the unit level will also be well documented.

If any Evaluation Flight is unsatisfactory, the candidate will return to their home unit for additional training. After additional training the candidate will fly that Evaluation Flight again with a different board member.

9.3 SIC LARGE AIRCRAFT

9.3.1 SECOND IN COMMAND

SIC'S must have at least the following:

1. Meet FAR 135.245 and FAR 121 Appendixes F.

2. Pilot card with SIC sign off

3. For initial, 5 mission training flights.

4. For recurrent, 1 refresher flight with Paracargo

9.4 SMOKEJUMPER INSTRUCTOR PILOTS

Agency Instructor Pilots must have at least the following:

- CFI, CFII, MEI
- 100 Hours in Make and Model
- Standardization Check Ride
- National Office Designation
- Biennial Standardization Workshop (USFS)

9.5 SMOKEJUMPER INSPECTOR PILOTS

- 3 Years Smokejumper Pilot Experience
- 100 Missions
- 1 Year Active Smokejumper Pilot Instructor
- National Office Designation
- Biennial Standardization Workshop and Checkride.

Inspectors will forward checkride records to the USFS and/or AMD where files will be retained.

9.6 CREW PILOT CARDING

Required flight crewmembers must have a USFS/USDI Smokejumper Pilot Checkride and signed pilot card issued within the previous 12 months authorizing them for smokejumper/Paracargo missions.

9.7 CURRENCY REQUIREMENTS

1. **All required Flight crewmembers** must have an annual refresher flight including Paracargo.

2. **Inspector and Instructor pilots** must be current Smokejumper captains in order to perform their tasks as instructors or inspectors and will be designated by the USFS or BLM National Aviation Office.

3. **All** required flight crewmembers and air crewmembers (DOI) must attend an approved CRM course every three years.

Chapter

10

10.0 Forms

10.1 USFS Checkride form

USFS SMOKEJUMPER PILOT EVALUATION AND APPROVAL RECORD

NAME OF PILOT (Last, First, M.I.)	LOCATION:	DATE OF CHECK:

NAME OF CHECK PILOT:	SPOTTER'S NAME:

PILOT CERTIFICATE INFORMATION:	TYPE A/C:	FLIGHT TIME:

PILOT MEDICAL INFORMATION:

GROUND PRE-FLIGHT BRIEFING/EXAM

GRADE DEFINITIONS: S - SATISFACTORY, U - UNSATISFACTORY

ORAL EXAM:	S	U	STREAMER DROPS:	S	U
1. Smokejumper procedures	☐	☐	28. Established altitude	☐	☐
2. Use of crew resource management	☐	☐	29. Altitude call out from radar altimeter	☐	☐
3. Spotter/dispatch communications	☐	☐	30. Appropriate airspeeds	☐	☐
4. Weight and balance	☐	☐	31. Appropriate streamer pattern for visual	☐	☐
5. Aircraft performance (DA, SE climb)	☐	☐	32. Appropriate call outs of streamers	☐	☐
6. Aircraft pre-flight inspection	☐	☐	33. Spotter communication	☐	☐
GROUND OPERATIONS:			34. Crew Resource Management	☐	☐
7. Engine start procedures	☐	☐	35. Use fo check list	☐	☐
8. Taxi operations	☐	☐	**DROPPING JUMPERS:**		
9. Spotter communications	☐	☐	36. Configuration and transition	☐	☐
10. Crew resource management	☐	☐	37. Jumper pattern	☐	☐
11. Use of check list	☐	☐	37a. General flight path	☐	☐
IN FLIGHT - ENROUTE:			37b. Appropriate bank angles	☐	☐
12. Radio set-up	☐	☐	37c. Call outs to spotter (altitudes and pattern	☐	☐
13. Airport traffic departure	☐	☐	37d. Line up on final	☐	☐
14. Long range navigation set up	☐	☐	37e. Adequate length final	☐	☐
15. Radio communications	☐	☐	37f. Corrections/coordinated/responsive	☐	☐
16. Spotter communications	☐	☐	37g. Airspeed control	☐	☐
17. Crew resource management	☐	☐	37h. Altitude	☐	☐
18. Use of check list	☐	☐	38. Spotter communication	☐	☐
ARRIVAL AT INCIDENT:			39. Crew resource management	☐	☐
19. Communication with ground and other aircraft	☐	☐	40. Use of check list	☐	☐
20. Establish jump spot identification	☐	☐	**CARGO:**		
21. Establish probable streamer altitude	☐	☐	41. Configuration and transition	☐	☐
22. Low pass if agreed on with spotter	☐	☐	42. Appropriate pattern	☐	☐
22a. Appropriate altitude	☐	☐	42a. Terrain	☐	☐
22b. Airspeed	☐	☐	42b. Wind	☐	☐
22c. Power management	☐	☐	42c. Land marks	☐	☐
23. Spotter communication	☐	☐	42d. Altitude	☐	☐
24. Crew resource management	☐	☐	42e. Airspeed	☐	☐
25. Use of check list	☐	☐	42f. Power management	☐	☐
26. Density Altitude	☐	☐	42g. Call outs	☐	☐
27. Emergencies	☐	☐	42h. Accuracy	☐	☐
RESULT OF CHECKRIDE:			43. Spotter communication	☐	☐
APPROVED ?			44. Crew resource management	☐	☐
			45. Use of check list	☐	☐
☐ YES ☐ NO			46. Emergencies	☐	☐

REMARKS:

PILOTS SIGNATURE:	CHECK PILOTS SIGNATURE:

3/15/06   55

SMOKEJUMPER PILOT TRAINING RECORD (Ref. 5709.16.27.2-Exhibit 01. VI.)

PILOT:

A/C TYPE:

CONTRACTOR:

FLIGHT TRAINING HRS:

INSTRUCTOR PILOT_____

INSTRUCTOR SPOTTER

GRADING	AIRCRAFT									
Grading System based on a 1 to 10 scoring system with 10 being a perfect score, 8 satisfactory, 6 improving, 4 and less unsatisfactory performance.	TIME									
	DATE									

SMOKEJUMPER PILOT / COPILOT										
1. Attitude										
2. Knowledge of Aircraft and Systems										
3. Weight and Balance										
4. Awareness to Instruction										
5. Ground Operation - Taxiing, etc.										
6. Procedures - Normal and Single Engine										
7. Aircraft control - Airspeed, Altitude, Bank										
8. Attention to Flying the Aircraft										
9. Pilot - Spotter Cooperation										
10. Streamer Patterns										
11. Jumper Runs (Live)										
12. Patience										
13. Maneuvering										
14. Moderate and Deep Canyon Work										
15. Pattern Selection to DZ										
16. Awareness of Airspeed										
17. Timing of Power and Flap Application										
18. Basic Cargo (Dry Runs)										
20. Live Cargo Runs										
OTHER										
21. High Recon										
22. Low Recon										
23. Approach and Escape Routes										
GENERAL										
25. Judgment										
26. Crew Coordination										
27. Equipment & Procedures Knowledge										
28. Preflight Preparation										
29. Dispatch and Launch										
30. Enroute Procedures										
31. Safety (Clearing, Situational Awareness etc.)										
32. Flight Following										
TRAINEES INITIALS										

RECOMMENDED FOR EVALUATION CHECKRIDE BY: (IF REQUIRED)

INSTRUCTOR REMARKS and SIGNATURES

OFFICE OF AIRCRAFT SERVICES

INTERAGENCY AIRPLANE PILOT QUALIFICATIONS AND APPROVAL RECORD

Contract No. _____

Rental Agreement No. _____

Name: Last	First	MI	Date of Birth	Home Telephone ( )

Home Address	City, State & Zip Code			

Employed By	Address	Telephone	Employed Since

Previous Employer	Address	Telephone	Period Employed

Medical Certificate: Class _____ Date _____ Limitations _____	Airman Certificate: No. _____ ATP _____ Coml _____ Instrument _____ SEL _____ MEL _____ SES _____ MES _____ CFI _____ Type Ratings _____	Aircraft to be Flown On This Contract:	Total PIC Hours in Make/Model

Total Pilot Time	
Pilot-in-Command (PIC), Airplane	
PIC, Single-Engine Airplane	
PIC, Multiengine Airplane	
PIC, Seaplane	
PIC, Cross-Country	
PIC Night	
Instrument Simulator or "Hood"	
PIC "Actual Weather"	
PIC Airplane: Last 12 Months	
PIC Airplane: Last 60 Days	
PIC "Fire Surveillance" Opns.	
PIC "Low-Level" Opns. (<500' AGL)	
PIC "Animal/Fowl Surveillance" Opns.	
PIC Aircraft over 12,500# Gr.Wt.	
PIC "Typical Terrain" (Over Mtns, Etc)	
PIC Airtanker/Dispensing Opns.	
PIC Turbo Prop Airplanes	
PIC Jet Airplanes	
PIC Turbine Powered Aircraft	
Takeoff/Landings Last 90 Days	
Night Takeoff/Landings Last 90 Days	

Other Aircraft for Which Pilot is Current for "Part 135" Operations:

Make/Model: _____ _____ _____ _____ _____

Total PIC: _____ _____ _____ _____ _____

PART 135 FLIGHT CHECK (Attach Info Copy(s))

(135 Flight Checks Must Cover Type of Operations Required by Contract)

Date	Make/Model Acft.	Total PIC in Make/Model	Type Flight Check
_____	_____	_____	VFR ( ) IFR ( ) IFR W/AP ( )
_____	_____	_____	VFR ( ) IFR ( ) IFR W/AP ( )
_____	_____	_____	VFR ( ) IFR ( ) IFR W/AP ( )

Date of Previous Agency Card Approval

OAS: _____ USFS: _____

Date of Last Agency Flight Check

OAS: _____ USFS: _____

Aircraft Accidents/FAA Violations Last 5 Years

(/ No / / Yes (Attach Date & Explanation)

Previous OAS or USFS Card Denied, Suspended, or Revoked?

(/ No / / Yes (Attach Explanation)

Airtanker Operations Only:

Date Last PIC IFR Check in Type _____ Date Last FAR 61.55 Copilot Check _____

I certify that the information listed on this form is true and correct. In addition, I certify that I have read the statements on the back of this form covering information pursuant to Public Law 93-579 (Privacy Act of 1974).

Date _____ Signature of Pilot _____

Special Use Operations

Duty Approved For: (Inspector Shall Initial)

_____ Low-Level (Less than 500 Ft. Above the Surface) (8D)

_____ Animal/Fowl, Surveillance/Control

_____ Mtn. Flying-Unimproved Strips (9A)

_____ Snow (Ski) Operations (4)

_____ Recon (USFS) _____

For Inspector's Use Only

_____ Airtanker Pilot (AT)

_____ Airtanker Pilot, "Initial Attack" (1A)

_____ Airtanker Copilot (CP)

_____ Agriculture Application

_____ Other _____

_____ Fire Surveillance

_____ Smokejumper (2E)

_____ Paracargo (9E)

_____ Aerial Ignition (8)

_____ Other _____

Authorized Operations:

SEL _____ SES _____ MEL _____ MES _____ IFR, W/CP _____ IFR, Single Pilot _____

Make/Model (Type) Aircraft	Inspector's Signature	Agency	Date	Expiration Date
_____	_____	_____	_____	_____
_____	_____	_____	_____	_____

Remarks: _____

OAS-64A (08/99) White-Contracting/Tech. Services Yellow-Inspector Green-Pilot

STATEMENT OF COMPETENCY

I certify that _____ has successfully completed the following proficiency
          (Pilot Name)
checks and meets all FAR 135 requirements for this company:

FIXED WING

Single Engine, VFR (135.293 a & b):

Date _____ Type A/C _____ Check Pilot _____ FAA (Office)
or Company _____

Multiengine, VFR (135.293 a & b):

Date _____ Type A/C _____ Check Pilot _____ FAA (Office)
or Company _____

IFR (135.297a):

Date _____ Type A/C _____ Check Pilot _____ FAA (Office)
or Company _____

Single Pilot IFR with Autopilot (135.297g):

Date _____ Type A/C _____ Check Pilot _____ FAA (Office)
or Company _____

Line/Route Check (135.299):

Date _____ Type A/C _____ Check Pilot _____ FAA (Office)
or Company _____

SIGNED: _____ DATE: _____
     (Chief Pilot or Manager)

COMPANY: _____

10.4 OAS 64D

OAS 64D (3/99)

PERSONNEL DATA INFORMATION AND PILOT CARDING

☐ Initial Employment with DOI
☐ Annual/Interim

Please provide all requested information.
Please provide your name, a copy of your medical certificate, your flight time for the last 12 months, your signature, and any information that has changed.

PERSONAL INFORMATION

Name:_____ Bureau/Agency:_____
      Last   First   MI

Office
Address:_____
      Street/P.O. Box   City   State   ZIP

Office Phone (_____)_____ Fax (_____)_____ E-mail _____

FOR EMERGENCY INFORMATION ONLY

Home
Address:_____
      Street/P.O. Box   City   State   ZIP

Home Phone (_____)_____

MEDICAL INFORMATION (Attach a copy of your medical certificate, required annually.)

AIRMAN CERTIFICATE INFORMATION (Attach a copy of initial employment.)

      Additional ratings obtained: _____

      Date of last Flight Review (FAR 61.56): _____

FLIGHT TIME INFORMATION

Total Pilot Time   _____

Total PIC Airplane	_____	**Last 12 months:**	
PIC Single-engine land	_____	**PIC Airplane**	_____
PIC Multiengine land	_____	**Special Use:**	
PIC Single-engine sea	_____	Low level	_____
PIC Multiengine sea	_____	Unprepared site	_____
Water T/O and Landings	_____	Smokejumper	_____
PIC Instrument (Actual)	_____	Other	_____
PIC Instrument (Sim / Hood)	_____	Other	_____
PIC Night	_____		
PIC Airplane over 12,000 Gross	_____		
Airplane instructor time	_____		

Total PIC Helicopter	_____	**Last 12 months:**	
PIC Helicopter (Recip)	_____	**PIC Helicopter**	_____
PIC Helicopter (Turbine)	_____	**Special Use:**	
PIC Instrument (Actual)	_____	Low level	_____
PIC Instrument (Sim / Hood)	_____	Bucket	_____
PIC Night	_____	Long line	_____
PIC Helicopter over 6,000 Gross	_____	Aerial ignition	_____
Helicopter instructor time	_____	Mountain	_____
		Other	_____
		Other	_____
		Other	_____

I certify that the information provided is true and correct.

_____   _____
Signature   **Date**

OAS 64D (3/99)

PRIVACY ACT NOTICE

GENERAL.-This information is provided pursuant to Public Law 93-579 (Privacy Act of 1974). December 31, 1974, for individuals supplying information for inclusion system of records.

AUTHORITY-The authority to collect the information on the attached form is contained in 5 USC 552A.

PURPOSES AND USE-This information, along with data you may have supplied previously, and information developed by investigation will be for use such as:

1. To determine your pilot qualifications to comply with contract specifications.
2. Transfer to the U.S. Department of Justice in the event of litigation.
3. Transfer, in the event there is indicated violation or potential violation of a statute, regulation, whether civil, criminal, or regulatory in nature, to the appropriate agency or agencies, whether federal, state, local, or foreign, changed with the responsibility of investigation or prosecuting such violation or charged with enforcing or implementing the statute, rule, regulation, order, or license violated or potentially violated.

For Inspector's Use Only

AIRPLANE PILOT CARD

SPECIAL USE APPROVAL: (Inspector shall initial.)

_____ Low Level	_____ Smokejumper	_____ Lead Plane/Air Attack
_____ Unprepared Site	_____ Aerial Ignition	_____ Other _____
_____ External Loads	_____ Airtanker Coordinator	_____ Other _____

AUTHORIZED OPERATIONS:

SEL_____   SES_____   MEL_____   MES_____   IFR W/CP_____   IFR Single Pilot_____

Aircraft Approved:	Inspector's Signature	Agency	Date	Expiration Date

Remarks: IFR Expiration Date _____

HELICOPTER PILOT CARD

SPECIAL USE APPROVAL: (Inspector shall initial.)

_____ Short Haul	_____ Low Level	_____ External Load
_____ Rappel	_____ Mountain Flying	_____ Long Line
_____ Deep Snow Landing	_____ Fire Suppression	_____ Animal Gathering/Capture (Device)
_____ Platform/Vessel Landing	_____ Retardant/Water Dropping	_____ Toe-in Single Skid, Stepout
_____ Animal Eradication/Tagging	_____ Aerial Ignition (Device)	_____ Other _____

Aircraft Approved:	Inspector's Signature	Agency	Date	Expiration Date

Remarks:

10.5 OAS 69

OAS-69 (03/85)			Circle One:	Interim	Initial	Recurrent	Post-Accident
USFS-5700	INTERAGENCY PILOT EVALUATION/QUALIFICATION CHECK				Date		

H-Helicopter	A-Airplane	D-Demonstrated Ability		K-Knowledge		U-Unsatisfactory	
Pilot's Name (Last, First, Middle Initial)				Knowledge Make & Model		Competency Make & Model	

Employed By:				Location of Check		Flight Time	

	EQUIPMENT EXAM - (Oral/Written)	////		e.	Short/Soft Field Landings	(A)	
1.	Aircraft/Pilot Documents			f.	Rejected Landings/Go-Around		
2.	Weight & Balance (Down Loading)			g.	Winter/Ski Operations/Snow Landings		
3.	Fuel Requirements			h.	STOL Operations	(A)	
4.	Systems Operation			i.	Pinnacle Or Platform	(H)	
5.	Emergency Procedures			j.	Confined Area	(H)	
6.	Emergency/Survival Equipment			k.	Slope Landing	(H)	
7.	Operations/Safety Briefing		8.		Emergency Procedures		////
	PREFLIGHT	////		a.	Engine Failure After TO		
1.	Aircraft Documents			b.	Maneuvering with Engine Out		
2.	Manifest and Flight Plan			c.	V-Speeds	(A)	
3.	Weight and Balance			d.	Approach & Landing, One Engine Out		
4.	Preflight Procedure			e.	System Emergencies		
5.	Use of Check List			f.	Autorotations/Forced Landings		
	FLIGHT CHECK	////		g.	Antitorque Failure	(H)	
1.	Starting Procedure			h.	Hydraulic Failure		
2.	Com. & Nav. Equipment Check		9.		Instrument Procedures		////
3.	Hover Taxi/Ground Taxi			a.	Equipment Check		
4.	Run-Up/Power Check			b.	ATC Procedures		
5.	Takeoff Operations	////		c.	Navigation/Orientation		
	a. Normal Takeoff			d.	Holding		
	b. Crosswind Takeoff			e.	Approach - NDB, VOR, DME, LOC, ILS		
	c. Maximum Performance Takeoff			f.	Missed Approach/Circling Approach		
	d. Short/Soft Field Takeoff	(A)		g.	Speed, Heading Altitudes		
	e. Aborted Takeoff			h.	Auto Pilot/Single Pilot	(A)	
6.	Air-Work Maneuvers	////		i.	Crew Coordination		
	a. Smoke-Hell Jumping/Rappelling		10.		Water Operations		////
	b. App. to Stall, Slow Flight			a.	Taxiing, Sailing, Docking		
	c. Mountain Flying Technique			b.	Step Taxi & Turns	(A)	
	d. Sling Operation/External Load			c.	Glassy Water/Rough Water		
	e. Water/Retardant Dropping			d.	Takeoff & Landings		
	f. Aerial Hunting		11.		Judgment		
	g. Offshore Navigation		12.		Shutdown Checklist		
	h. Horse and Game Hrdg/Cntg	(H)			REMARKS/LIMITATIONS		
	i. Night Operation						
	j. Low-Level Operations						
	k. Fire Recon						
	l. Steep Turns						
	m. En Route Procedures						
7.	Approach Landing	////					
	a. Wind Evaluation						
	b. Helispot Evaluation	(H)			PILOT QUALIFICATION CARD ISSUED FOR:		
	c. Normal (Wheel/Stall)						
	d. Crosswind/Slip Approach						

Pilot Statement: I have been briefed on the reason for this evaluation flight and understand that I will remain as pilot-in-command of the aircraft during the check and that I may refuse to attempt any maneuver which, in my opinion, may be hazardous or unsafe.

_____ Approved   _____ Disapproved (See Remarks)

Expiration Date: _____

_____
Pilot's Signature (Sign Prior to Flight)

IFR _____   VFR _____

_____
Inspector's Signature

GLOSSARY

<u>AFF</u> - Automated Flight Following.

<u>AGL</u> - Above Ground Level.

<u>AIR TACTICAL GROUP SUPERVISOR ATGS</u> - Specially trained fireman who rides in a chase plane to direct retardant drops over
fires. The AAB is responsible for air traffic control and for
setting mission priorities. In his absence, the smokejumper
spotter assumes the responsibilities of the AAE.

<u>AMD</u> – Aviation Management Directorate. The agency formerly known as the OAS.
<u>AREA</u> - BLM administrative sub division of a District.

<u>ASM</u> - Aerial Supervision Module, consisting of a "ATCO" or Leadplane Pilot and an Air Attack operating as a team.

<u>BLM -</u> Bureau of Land Management. A Bureau of the Department of the Interior, which among other responsibilities, is responsible for suppression of wildfires on most of Alaska's federal land.

<u>BURNING CONDITIONS</u> - The combined conditions of fuel moisture, temperature, wind, humidity, etc., which effects how intensely wildfires will burn on a given day. Burning conditions, alongwith lightning forecasts, directly effect the degree of readiness maintained by the smokejumper project, specifically standby assignments.

<u>CANOPY</u> - The material and lines that make up what is usually identified as a parachute. Does not include container, D-bag, and other components of a parachute system.

<u>CARGO DROP AIRSPEED</u> - The airspeed an aircraft must fly to safely drop cargo.

<u>CHARGE CODE</u> - A multi-digit computer number associated with all expenditures of BLM funds which keys the money spent to the program and activity it was spent for.

<u>CHASE PLANE</u> - Same as a lead plane. This term is probably more appropriate in Alaskan style air attack operations.

<u>CONVECTION</u> COLUMN - Towering column of smoke which may rise thousands of feet in the air over a fire.
<u>COORDINATES</u> - Latitude and longitude locations to the nearest minute which is the primary method used to describe the location of fires in Alaska.

CORRECTION - Left or right changes in aircraft heading accomplished with bank turns in 5 degree increments, at the direction of the spotter on final approach to the jump spot or exit point. Corrections of greater magnitude than 5 degrees are accomplished with quick banked turns when requested.

DEMOBE - The retrieval of smokejumpers and other firefighters from a fire.

DETECTION - Activities that focus on locating new fires at the earliest possible moment.

DISTRICT - Administrative sub-division in the BLM organization; in Alaska, there are two Districts: Fairbanks District and Anchorage District.

DOI - Department of the Interior.

DRIFT - The distance streamers drift down-wind from their release point.

DROGUE - A static line deployed stabilization parachute used with ram air canopies

DROP ZONE (DZ) - Term similar to jump spot, but usually used in reference to cargo drop areas.

DRY RUN Term sometimes used to mean dummy run, though usually used to refer to a smokejumper mission that did not drop jumpers on a fire.

DUMMY PASS - Practice cargo run pattern in which cargo is not dropped for the purpose of letting the pilot determine the suitability of his selected run.

ECON CRUISE - Normal power setting speed used by smokejumper aircraft returning from fire runs, flying point to point, or on patrols (fuel-efficient operations).

EFF CREW - Generally, a crew of 16 drawn from a native village, trained in fire suppression, and hired as needed for a specific fire.

EFF - Emergency Fire Fighters hired day to day to meet a fire emergency.

EMT - Emergency Medical Technician. The smokejumper project maintains approximately 12 EMT's for rescue and emergency medical care of injured firefighters.

EXIT POINT – For round canopies a point equal distance up-wind of the jump spot as the streamers landed down-wind and over which the jumpers must exit the aircraft to compensate for the wind drift in their parachutes. For square parachutes this may be up to twice the distance up wind as determined by the spotter.

EXIT - the procedure used by smokejumpers to jump from an aircraft.

EXTENDED STANDBY-Normally thought as the hours assigned beyond the normal 8 hour day.

FAST CRUISE - Maximum power setting speed used by smokejumper aircraft enroute to initial attack fires with an eye toward speed and not fuel economy.

FIRE PACK - A pre-packed box containing food, shelter, and fire fighting tools for two smokejumpers pre-rigged for cargo drop.

FUEL TYPE - Classification of various types of trees, brush, tundra, etc., in order to describe burning characteristics, or probabilities of a fire.

GO AROUND - An aborted live run.

HARNESS - The webbing strap arrangement that a jumper wears to which his parachute is attached.

HELITACK - Firefighters whose primary means of transportation to fires is by helicopter and who are specifically trained in helicopter procedures.

INITIAL ATTACK - The critical first attack on a new fire with the objective of containing it while it is small.

JUMP SPOT - The area on the ground selected by the spotter as the most desirable area for smokejumpers to land from the standpoint of safety and tactical advantage to attack the fire.

KICKER - A smokejumper assigned in charge of para cargo missions to accomplish the actual dropping of cargo bundles out the open door of the aircraft.

LEAD PLANE - A fast maneuverable light twin-engine aircraft used by the AAB to make low passes over desired targets for retardant, to lead retardant bombers to a target, and to follow, or chase, retardant bombers while they make their drop and observe the drop effectiveness.

LIVE RUN - A flight pattern on which jumpers or cargo will be dropped after streamer runs or dummy runs.

LOAD - The crew of smokejumpers carried by smokejumper aircraft with a standard amount of initial attack cargo.

LOFT - The facilities used for packing and repairing the parachutes. Consists of packing table room, drying tower, and sewing machines.

LOW PASS - A low and slow pass made along side a fire to help the spotter size-up the fire and select a jump spot.

MAIN - Primary parachute assembly used for intentional jumps.

MODIFICATION - Series of holes cut in the rear of a parachute to give the parachute forward speed and turning ability to allow it to be maneuvered.

MOP-UP - The procedure of digging up and putting out a fire after the fire has been contained.

MSL - Mean Sea Level.

OAS 2 or 23 - Pay documents which are filled out after each flight and each day with appropriate charge codes from which the basis of payment to contractors for aircraft availability and flight time.

OAS 2 - Flight log document which is filled out after each flight and each day with appropriate charge codes for finance coding, aircraft maintenance coding, and pilot times are derived for fleet aircraft.

OAS - office of Aircraft Services. A sister agency to the BLM under the Department of the Interior with responsibility for contracting and regulating aircraft used by Department of Interior agencies.

OPERATIONS - Smokejumper operations is responsible for readiness of smokejumpers and aircraft to respond to fires. Smokejumper pilots and aircraft receive their assignments from operations.

PROJECT FIRE - A large fire that has escaped initial attack and which is fought by a force of 80 or more firefighters over an extended period of time.

RESERVE - Auxiliary chest mounted parachute for use in the event of a malfunction of the main parachute.

RETARDANT - Liquid chemicals dropped from retardant bombers to slow the spread of a fire.

RIGGER - An FAA licensed parachute packer and repairman. Selected smokejumpers receive training as riggers.

SMOKEJUMPER DROP AIRSPEED - The airspeed the aircraft must fly for safe jumper exits and parachute deployment.

SMOKEJUMPER DROP ALTITUDE - The altitude ACL that the aircraft must fly to safely drop jumpers.

SMOKEJUMPER - An experienced professional fireman who is trained to parachute into wildfires in remote areas and in rugged terrain.

SPOTTER - A senior smokejumper who is trained to be in-charge of smokejumper missions.

STACK - The formation of aircraft separated vertically at 500 foot intervals over a fire for the purpose of air traffic control.

STAFFING - Term used for both the number of people and aircraft assigned to standby on a given day and for the process of delivering firefighters to a fire.

STANDBY - Standby is assigned to pilots by operations at the request of FMOs and is determined by burning conditions and lightning forecasts.

STATIC LINE - Line attached from the main parachute to the static line cable in the jump aircraft which activates the parachute as a jumper falls away.

STREAMERS - Twenty foot long weighted crepe paper strips that descend at the same rate as a personnel parachute that used by a spotter to help him determine wind drift.

TAWS – Terrain Awarness Warning System, a GPS based Ground Proximity Warning System required on all Turbine aircraft by March of 2005.

TCAS – Terminal Collision Avoidance System, required on all Smokejumper Aircraft.

UNIT - BLM administrative sub-division of an Area.

WEAK LINK - A short piece of 500 lb. tensile strength webbing with a ring attached. The weak link breaks in the event a static line cargo bundle becomes entangled in the static line. The purpose of the weak line is to protect the aircraft from excessive forces on the static line cable.

INDEX

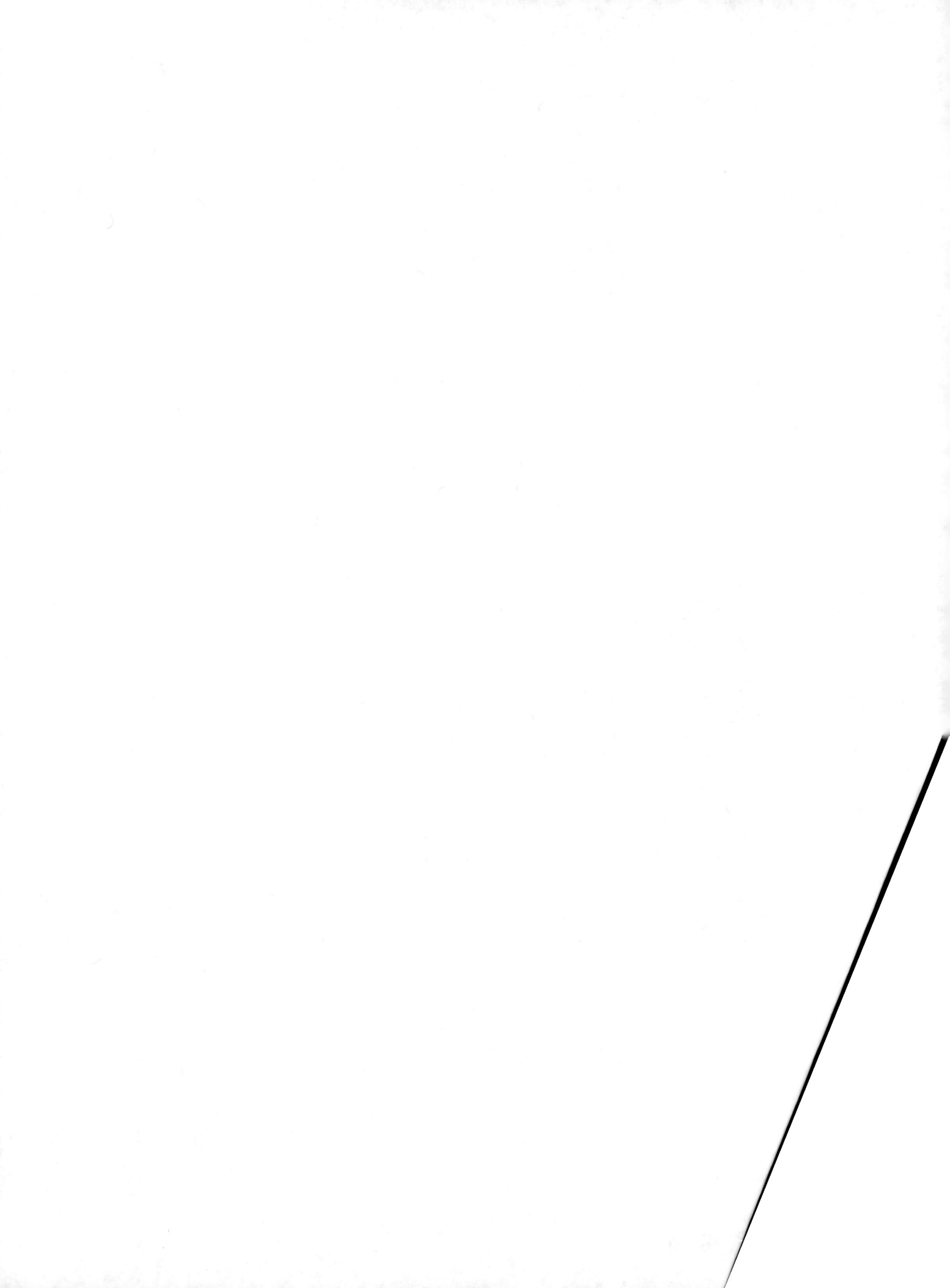